KEEPING
KOI

Comprehensive coverage, from building
a koi pond to choosing colour varieties.

Keith Holmes • Tony Pitham • Nick Fletcher

INTERPET PUBLISHING

CONTENTS

© 2005 Interpet Publishing,
Vincent Lane, Dorking, Surrey,
RH4 3YX, England.
All rights reserved.

ISBN: 1-84286-106-9

Credits
Created and compiled: Ideas
into Print, Claydon, Suffolk
IP6 0AB, England.
Design and prepress: Stuart
Watkinson, Ayelands, New Ash
Green, Kent DA3 8JW, England.
Practical photography: Geoff
Rogers © Interpet Publishing.
Production management:
Consortium, Poslingford, Suffolk
CO10 8RA, England.
Print production: Sino Publishing
House Ltd., Hong Kong.

Printed and bound in China.

Part Two: Building a koi pond 34-71

Authors

Keith Holmes & Tony Pitham have a wealth of experience in all aspects of the koi hobby, from pond building to koi health and appreciation. Tony is a frequent visitor to Japan to purchase high-grade koi and is a regular judge at the Shinkokai All-Japan Show. Both write regularly for koi magazines worldwide. They have prepared Parts 1-3.

Nick Fletcher, former editor of the UK aquatic monthly Practical Fishkeeping, regularly contributes articles to this and other fish-related publications. Nick is actively involved in his local koi club. He has prepared Part 4.

Other contributors:

Bernice Brewster
Mick Martin

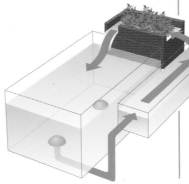

CONTENTS

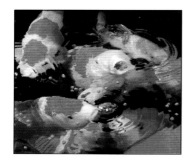

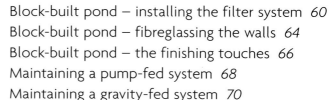

Part Three: Koi care and maintenance 72-105

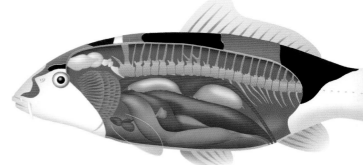

Part Four: Koi colour varieties 106-195

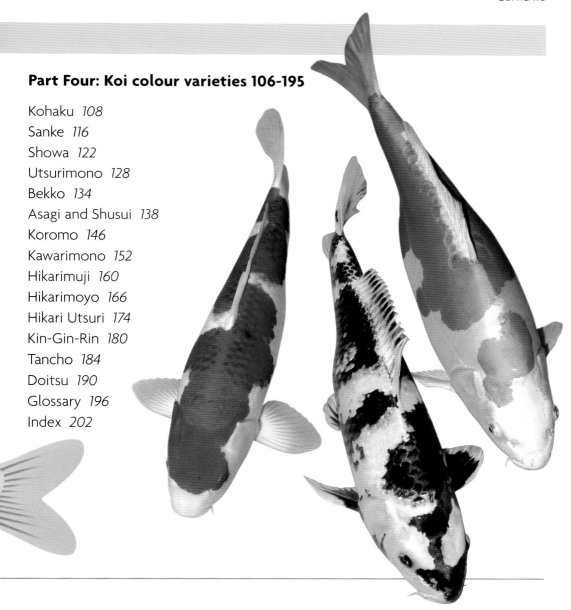

PART ONE

Getting the water right

If you are reading this book, you probably already have some form of pond, but you have been bitten by the 'koi bug' and are ready to accept the challenge of becoming a koi-keeper. Uppermost in your mind will be a desire to build a stunning pond in which to house your future collection of these magnificent ornamental fish. But do not rush! Building a koi pond raises a vast array of questions that you need to answer long before you start digging a hole in your garden. These are covered in the section starting on page 34.

In the natural environment, water is filtered as it passes over the gravel and stones of the substrate, and the toxins that are present are broken down by bacteria that flourish on the substrate surface. To keep fish in an enclosed system, we need to emulate their natural habitat as closely as possible, which means passing water through a suitable filter medium in order to cultivate colonies of the same oxygen-loving bacteria that will remove the harmful toxins.

Good filtration and water quality are vital if koi are to remain healthy all year round. The opening section of this book explores the bewildering variety of equipment designed to keep the water in good condition, from filters and media to pumps, valves, pipes and heating systems.

You can choose from a number of filtration systems in a wide range of shapes and sizes, each with their own individual features. Choosing the correct system can be a difficult decision, especially if you are on a limited budget. Remember that this will be the single most important purchase that you are likely to make when constructing your dream pond and any mistake could be extremely costly in the long run. As with the design of your pond, research this aspect thoroughly before you decide which system is best for you.

If you are unsure, do seek advice from friendly hobbyists or speak to your local koi dealer, who will be more than willing to offer guidance on technical and fish-related topics.

What is water quality?

Koi-keepers often say (as do all fishkeepers) that if you look after the water, the koi will look after themselves and, in many ways, there is much truth in this statement. Water quality varies according to its use; for example, drinking water is of excellent quality, but the chlorine content renders it unsuitable for fish. Numerous factors contribute to water quality and they interact with each other, so there is no simple definition of the term. With regard to koi-keeping, water quality is almost exclusively concerned with physical and chemical characteristics such as temperature, dissolved oxygen levels, pH, the nitrogenous waste produced by the fish, alkalinity, phosphate levels, particulate organic substances and dissolved organic substances.

Today's koi-keepers can choose from a wide range of filtration equipment to keep the water clean and wholesome. The options are described in detail on pages 10-33.

Right: Water conditioners can remove chlorine and other harmful tapwater contaminants. Many brands have a measuring device built into the container, enabling you to administer the exact dose. Mix the conditioner with pond water in a watering can and sprinkle it onto the pond surface or into the surface skimmer.

Above: Water purifiers are commonly installed on the incoming water supply of many koi ponds. Modern purifiers have the capacity to remove contaminants such as metals, in addition to chlorine and its derivatives. There are many different types available, so be sure to select the right type of water purifier based on a water report for your local area.

Reverse osmosis

In normal osmosis (right), water molecules pass across a partially permeable membrane from a dilute solution to a more concentrated one. With reverse osmosis, water pressure is used to reverse this flow.

Tapwater enters the reverse osmosis unit.

Mains pressure forces water through the membrane.

A partially permeable membrane allows only water molecules through.

Left over water can be used on the garden.

Pure water is drained from the unit.

Ideal water conditions for koi

For koi to flourish in your pond, follow these guidelines for water quality and make sure that:

● The water is free from contaminants. You must ensure that pond water is not polluted by external agents, such as chlorine, chloramine, fertilisers, pesticides and weedkillers.

● The water contains all the necessary trace elements, vitamins and minerals required for health, growth and reproduction.

● The water is well oxygenated. Using airpumps and venturis, as well as waterfalls in the hotter months of the year, will all help to improve oxygen levels in the pond water.

● The water is at a suitable temperature to ensure that the fishes' immune and metabolic systems are operating efficiently to keep infection at bay. A heating system helps to achieve and maintain a minimum acceptable temperature.

● The water is clear. Koi are happy in green (not dirty) water. It helps to improve skin quality and coloration, but if it becomes too green, you cannot see the fish and may miss signs of developing health problems.

● The water is adequately buffered to prevent large swings of pH (see water testing page 98).

What type of filter?

The filter system you choose will depend on whether you favour a pump-fed or gravity-fed system (see page 42), how much space you have available, how much you want to spend and your preference about the design and specification. Here, we discuss filters based on their size and form.

Single chamber filters

These filters consists of one chamber, normally made from a plastic tank and supplied with a combination of media. The incoming water is pumped through a spraybar at the top of the unit. They offer more of a 'quick fix' than a long-term solution, and are not suited to the demands of a koi pond. This is principally due to the fact that they are pump fed (i.e. supplied with water from a submersible pump in the pond) and the media inside the filter body cannot handle the waste loads put on them by koi.

Multichamber filters

These consist of between three and eight chambers. Their main advantage is that you can place different filter media in each chamber. Thus, in the first chamber it is normal to have a medium, such as brushes, that is good at straining out heavy waste, and in the last chamber a medium designed to trap very fine particles in a 'water polishing' final stage. The chambers in between can contain various types of media, mainly to carry out biological filtration.

Multichamber filters are normally made from heavy-duty plastic or fibreglass and in most cases incorporate drainage points on each chamber for the easy removal of waste. Multichamber units offer an ideal starting point when you are choosing a filter system for your new koi pond. The only drawback is that they are moulded as one unit and those with several chambers take up a large space in the garden.

Single box pump-fed filter

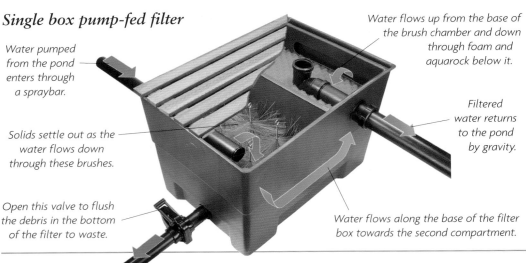

Water pumped from the pond enters through a spraybar.

Solids settle out as the water flows down through these brushes.

Open this valve to flush the debris in the bottom of the filter to waste.

Water flows up from the base of the brush chamber and down through foam and aquarock below it.

Filtered water returns to the pond by gravity.

Water flows along the base of the filter box towards the second compartment.

Multichamber pump-fed filter

The water flows over the next partition into the third chamber, typically containing aquarock.

Water pumped from the pond is aerated by a venturi.

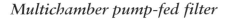

The water flows under the first partition into the second chamber, which could contain flocor.

Filtered water returns to the pond by gravity.

DIRECTION OF WATER FLOW

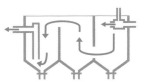

Drain valves to flush waste from the filter chambers.

Multichamber gravity-fed filter

Water flows into the filter under gravity.

A pump in the last chamber or an external one pulls water through the filter and back to the pond.

DIRECTION OF WATER FLOW

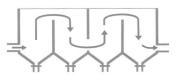

Typical filter media would be Japanese matting.

Waste drains from each chamber.

11

What type of filter?

Vortex chambers

These are not complete filter systems on their own, but they do offer an efficient way of dealing with heavy waste in the initial stages of filtration. If you are serious about keeping koi, you should definitely include a vortex chamber in your filter setup.

A vortex chamber is a very simple filter unit that makes use of a natural physical force. In the koi world, a vortex chamber consists of a cylinder – the bigger the better – in which a circulating flow of water is created by introducing the water at an angle so that it strikes the inner curved surface of the cylinder. The aim in a vortex chamber is to create a very slow-moving circulation so that any solid particles held in suspension settle out by gravity and collect in the base of the chamber. To facilitate the settlement process, the bottom section of the chamber is shaped into a funnel that leads down to a central drain. Opening a valve connected to this allows the accumulated waste to be flushed away. The larger the vessel, the further the water has to travel before it moves into the next filtration chamber. It is important to control the flow rate from your pump to achieve the most efficient settlement of waste in a vortex chamber; the higher the flow rate, the less efficient the unit becomes.

Because of how it works, a vortex chamber operates best as the first part of a gravity-fed filter system, in which water flows slowly from the pond into the filter through a large-bore pipe. If it was part of a pump-fed filter system, the higher pressure of the incoming water would set up too fast a spin in the vortex chamber for there to be any useful settlement effect. Also, the swirling current could disturb any solid waste that did collect in the base.

Vortex chamber

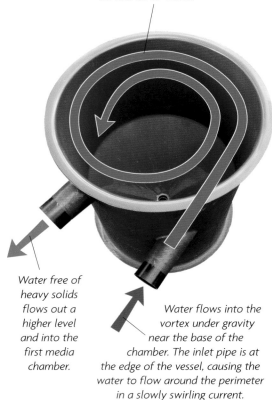

Heavy particles fall out of suspension at the centre and edges of the water flow and collect at the base, from where they can be flushed to waste.

Water free of heavy solids flows out a higher level and into the first media chamber.

Water flows into the vortex under gravity near the base of the chamber. The inlet pipe is at the edge of the vessel, causing the water to flow around the perimeter in a slowly swirling current.

Multichamber filters with a vortex

A vortex chamber can be used in conjunction with a multichamber filter system in two ways. It can be an integral part of a moulded unit or simply added as a separate 'front end' to a multichamber system. The advantages of using a built-in vortex are that no additional pipework is needed and installation is straightforward. However, such a system may be awkwardly long. Adding a separate vortex does at least allow for a degree of flexibility in positioning it in relation to the main filter unit.

However it is incorporated, a vortex brings the same benefits in removing a large amount of solid waste and thus freeing up one of the subsequent chambers and its media to do another job. The efficient removal of solid waste not only reduces maintenance on the other filter chambers – only the vortex will need regular draining – but it also allows one more chamber to contain a much-needed biological filter medium (see page 16).

Multichamber filter with built-in vortex

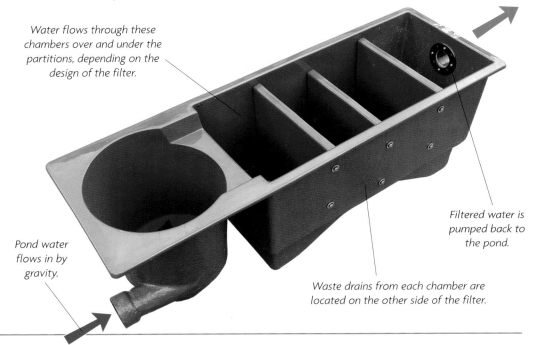

Water flows through these chambers over and under the partitions, depending on the design of the filter.

Pond water flows in by gravity.

Filtered water is pumped back to the pond.

Waste drains from each chamber are located on the other side of the filter.

13

What type of filter?

Multichamber vortex filters

These are moulded units with cylindrical vortex-like chambers rather than the more usual square or rectangular ones. Although the media contained in the chambers will prevent a vortex water flow, many people consider that using cylindrical chambers prevents dead spots that can impede good flow in more conventional designs.

Multiple single chambers

This is the most flexible option, enabling you to configure your own filter system from individual chambers linked together. It is best to choose vortex chambers, even though only one will be used as such. The main disadvantage in this approach is that you will need to connect the chambers with the necessary pipework and valves. However, the overwhelming bonus is that you can position the chambers to suit your space. If you have an L-shaped area available in your garden, you can arrange the units in the same way. And, of course, you can add more units to increase the filter capacity as you increase the size or stocking level of your pond.

An added benefit is that you can control the flow of water through the system. Ideally, it is best to have the water flowing up through the medium in each chamber, whereas in premoulded multichamber systems you are restricted to the flow pattern provided by the manufacturer.

Final thoughts on filters

Here we have considered the main types of filters available although, of course, there are many variations. At this point, it is probably clear to you that the best option is to choose a gravity-fed filter system incorporating a vortex chamber. If your pond

Right: *Colourful, healthy koi swimming in crystal clear water is the dream of all koi-keepers. Installing the right type and capacity of filter system will help to ensure that the fish flourish and grow.*

Multiple single chambers

This chamber contains Japanese matting as a biological filter medium.

The first empty chamber acts as a vortex.

The third chamber also contains Japanese matting.

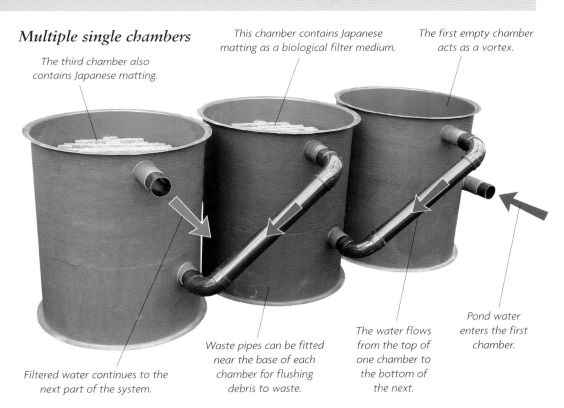

Filtered water continues to the next part of the system.

Waste pipes can be fitted near the base of each chamber for flushing debris to waste.

The water flows from the top of one chamber to the bottom of the next.

Pond water enters the first chamber.

has two bottom drains (see page 47), it is worth installing a separate filter system for each drain. This will enable you to carry out vital maintenance work on one system while keeping the other one running. It will also give you a backup should a pump fail in one of the systems. You may think that installing two filters seems extravagant, but at least each one can be smaller than a single one.

Whatever type of filter system you choose for your pond, be sure to allow enough room for it in your garden. The classic mistake is to build a pond with a capacity of 45,000 litres (10,000 gallons) and then realise that you will need a quarter of that area for a suitable filter. Do your homework first and you will have a filter system that is efficient, not too obtrusive and easy to maintain.

What type of filter media?

At the same time as deciding which type of filter system to install, you should also be thinking about the filter media to use. There are many types available but all perform one or both of the following functions:

Mechanical filtration – literally trapping solid wastes and removing them from the water flow.

Biological filtration – providing a large surface area to support the growth of beneficial bacteria that break down pollutants in the water.

Before finally choosing the media, consider the following questions. What job does the medium do best? Will it trap solids or foster biological filtration

by supporting millions of beneficial bacteria? The answers to these crucial questions will guide you in placing each medium in the most appropriate stage of the filter system. Also consider how easy the medium is to work with. Is it heavy and will this put you off cleaning it? And remember to think about the amount of media you will need; a large pond may require a substantial amount of filter media to keep it clean. Also make sure that the direction of water flow through your system matches the way the particular medium works best. With these questions buzzing around in your mind, the photos and associated captions here provide a visual survey of the filter media you will find at your local koi centre. If you are still unsure, your dealer will advise you on the best media for your particular system.

Pieces of ribbed plastic pipe provide a lightweight biological and mechanical filter medium.

These ribbed plastic balls also provide a large surface area for beneficial bacteria.

These sintered clay pieces (Aquarock) are an efficient, but heavy, biological medium.

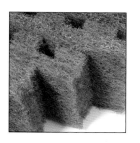

Left: Japanese matting sheets cut and assembled into 'cartridges' are one of the best types of biological filter medium available.

Below: Matala is a more rigid material than matting and is supplied in different grades. It can be used for mechanical as well as biological filtration.

Filter media combinations

A typical pump-fed multichamber system without a vortex could have the following sequence of media.

| Brushes | Plastic pieces | Japanese matting | Foam or Matala plus Aquarock |

A gravity-fed system with a vortex could follow the same sequence, but the vortex normally makes the brushes unnecessary. The following media setup is considered by many koi-keepers to be the best.

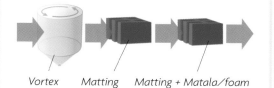

Vortex   Matting   Matting + Matala/foam

Filter foam needs frequent cleaning but can help to improve water clarity.

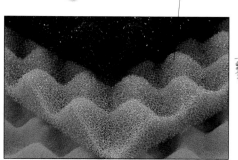

Brushes are an inexpensive, easy-to-clean mechanical filter medium. Available in a range of sizes.

Choosing pipes and valves

The pond and filter system are connected by pipework and it is vital to choose the correct types and sizes of pipes and valves to get your system running in the most efficient and reliable way. You will also need to consider where the pipework will run, whether it will be above or below the ground, have a long distance to run and be under pressure. Here we look at the options available and how to make the right choices from the outset.

Flexible hose

Flexible hose is the cheapest and most versatile type of pipework and is available in a range of bore sizes from 3 to 50mm (0.125-2in), although 38mm (1.5in) is normally the largest size used for koi ponds. The main advantages of flexible hose are that it is supplied in long lengths (normally up to 30m/100ft) and can easily cope with corners and irregular shapes. On the downside, it cannot be fitted with the valves and accessories widely used in the koi hobby and is normally used only where rigid pipework is unsuitable. A less serious problem is that flexible hoses can look very unsightly once they are installed.

Rigid pipework

Rigid plastic pipework is the best type to use for koi pond installations, especially gravity-fed systems. Using the right type and size of rigid pipework – normally the solvent-weld waste pipe – you can create a durable, efficient and 'professional-looking' system. Avoid using plastic pipework with push-fit connectors that are sealed with a rubber 'O' ring; these cannot handle high water pressures.

Above: Double union ball valves are used before and after this external pump. They will allow the pump to be replaced without cutting into the solvent-welded pipework around it.

82mm (3in). Used for drains

110mm (4in). Used for drains

50mm (2in). Used for returns

38mm (1.5in). Used for returns

Using pipework

Whatever type of pipework you choose, always follow these simple rules:

Use the right pipe

Ensure that you use the correct type and size of pipe for each part of the system and that the pipes can handle the volume of water you want to put through them.

Do a dry run first

Before gluing solvent-weld connections, place the pipes and valves in position in a 'dry run' and mark all the pipework clearly. You can never separate glued joints.

Match special components

If you are using any specialist equipment, such as sophisticated pumps and filtration devices, follow the manufacturer's recommendations for suitable pipework diameters. Generally speaking, the larger the pipe diameter, the lower the resistance and thus the lower the flow loss.

Use plenty of valves

Fit as many valves as possible so that you can isolate and replace faulty pumps and other devices without having to cut pipework. Fit a valve (normally a 110mm/4in slide or ball valve) before the filter so that you can isolate it from the pond for maintenance and purging pipes.

Double union ball valve

Regulates flow and has a threaded fitting (or union) on both sides so that it can be disconnected from the pipework.

Slide valve

Ideal for off/on functions, such as waste drainage. Only removable by cutting pipework or dismantling the valve.

Green clear reinforced /Heavy duty black hose

Stronger than normal reinforced hose and ideal for applications where it needs to be buried.

Clear hose

Transparent plastic hose is prone to kinking. It also allows sunlight to penetrate, causing algae growth that blocks the pipe.

Black-ribbed reinforced hose

This is very strong and does not kink around bends. Being black, it does not allow algae growth to build up.

19

Choosing a pump

Whether you choose a submersible or external water pump depends on how your final system will run.

Submersible pumps

Submersible pumps are used underwater, either in the pond for a pump-fed system or in the last chamber of the filter system on a gravity-fed pond. Submersible pumps are widely available, relatively inexpensive, very easy to install and can have a warranty period of up to five years. However, since the pump is located in the pond or the last filter chamber, cleaning entails removing the unit, which can be time consuming, especially for pumps in the pond, where they are exposed to dirty water and liable to clog. Submersibles with a pre-filter foam need regular maintenance to keep them running efficiently. In the pond, submersible pumps can be an obstacle on which koi could damage themselves. In the last filter chamber, they take up media space.

External pumps

For a gravity-fed pond, an external pump is the best choice. The pump is placed after the filter system and so pumps clean filtered water back to the pond. This cuts down on maintenance and also makes access easy should any attention be necessary.

High-wattage external pump

Pumped water outflow to pond or other treatment equipment.

Pump motor

Strainer basket prevents solids damaging pump impeller.

Water inlet from filter or surface skimmer.

Mount external pumps in a dry, sheltered place.

Sump, or cellar, pump

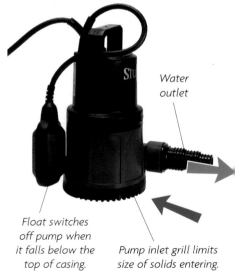

Water outlet

Float switches off pump when it falls below the top of casing.

Pump inlet grill limits size of solids entering.

Submersible pump

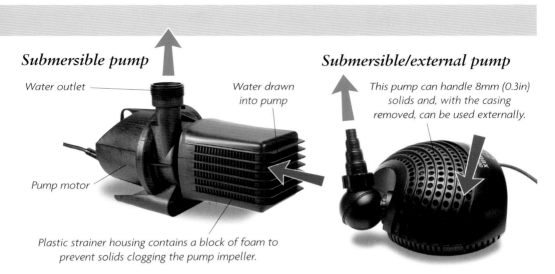

Water outlet

Water drawn into pump

Pump motor

Plastic strainer housing contains a block of foam to prevent solids clogging the pump impeller.

Submersible/external pump

This pump can handle 8mm (0.3in) solids and, with the casing removed, can be used externally.

Single-purpose external pumps must be sited under cover or in a weatherproof housing. Dual-purpose external pumps are usually smaller and when used out of the water are able to withstand wet weather. However, they may not be powerful enough to move high volumes of water or able to maintain the water pressure to operate some equipment.

Always choose a pump that will maintain a sufficient flow rate. Ideally, you will want to turn the whole pond volume over once every two hours. Check that it can cope with the flow loss caused by the height the water needs to reach and restrictions caused by the pipework. It must be able to maintain the pressure necessary to operate all the 'extras' that you may wish to connect to your system.

Low-wattage pumps, although more expensive to buy, are cheaper to run. However, these may not generate the pressure you require and you will need a bigger model to achieve the optimum flow rate.

Low-wattage external pump

These pumps are relatively cheap to run but do not deliver the same pressure as high-wattage models.

Water outflow

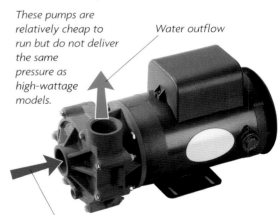

Water inlet. Normally a strainer basket is fitted here.

Heating a koi pond

Pond heating has become part of the wider koi hobby, partly because the equipment is now more widely available and reasonably priced. In addition, most of the koi now being imported into cool temperate regions have not experienced the conditions of an unheated pond in the cold winter months. By 'pond heating' we mean maintaining a minimum temperature of 12-14°C (54-57°F).

Heating reduces dangerous fluctuations in temperature and allows the koi to feed all year. In the long term it could prevent many problems and safeguard the health of a potentially prize-winning collection. After all, the value of one good-quality koi could cover the cost of a simple heating system.

How to heat the water? There are two types of heating system widely used to heat a koi pond: direct electric heating and secondary systems using a heat exchanger connected to a gas or oil-fired boiler.

Direct electric heating

This is the easiest heating system to install and generally takes the form of an inline electric heater fitted in the pipe returning water to the pond in a gravity-fed system. Where an external pump is used, the heater would normally be positioned after the pump. Depending on the ambient temperature of the water, allow one kilowatt of electrical power per 4,500 litres (1,000 gallons) of pond capacity. Ideally, choose the next most powerful heater so that it is not permanently on during severe and protracted periods of cold weather.

Choose a model with a digital thermostat. These offer more precise control over the heating process and provide an accurate readout of the current water temperature. If you are not experienced, engage a qualified electrician to install any type of electric heating system.

Inline electric water heater

Efficient and simple to install, electric heaters are the easiest option for water heating.

The power lead connects to this unit, which in some models also houses the timer and thermostat.

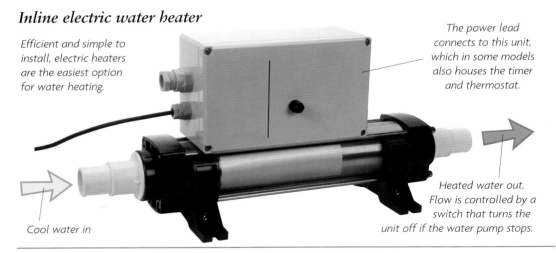

Cool water in

Heated water out. Flow is controlled by a switch that turns the unit off if the water pump stops.

Heat exchanger for gas-fired boiler

A heat exchanger supplied with hot water from a boiler is a very cost-effective way of heating pond water. The exchanger is best mounted vertically.

Heat exchanger systems

Although more expensive to buy and install, systems that use a heat exchanger are more economical in terms of running costs, particularly on larger ponds. The heat exchanger – normally made of stainless steel – is literally a radiator that is fed with hot water heated in a boiler, which can be fuelled by gas, oil or bottled gas. Pond water is pumped through the exchanger and heated by conduction as it passes over the hot water element inside. Water temperature is monitored by a probe in the pond connected to a digital thermostat that fires up the heating boiler when needed. If it is powerful enough, you can run the exchanger from your domestic heating system. Consult a qualified engineer to install such a system and take specialist advice if you plan to connect the pond heating setup to your home system.

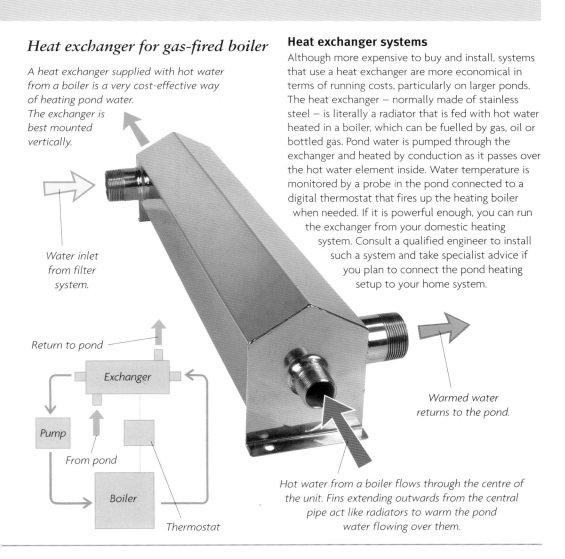

Water inlet from filter system.

Return to pond

Exchanger

Pump

From pond

Boiler

Thermostat

Warmed water returns to the pond.

Hot water from a boiler flows through the centre of the unit. Fins extending outwards from the central pipe act like radiators to warm the pond water flowing over them.

Surface skimmers and aeration systems

In addition to the main filtration system, there are many other items of equipment that you can add to your koi pond to improve water quality and facilitate maintenance. Here we look at the range of options available and explain briefly how they work.

Surface skimmers

A surface skimmer is an absolute must, rather than an optional extra. This unit literally skims the top layer of water and removes leaves, dust and other debris floating on the surface. The most effective type of skimmer is built into the pond wall and so must be installed early in the construction phase. An external pump – either the main one or a dedicated one – pulls water through a strainer basket in the unit by drawing water into the mouth of the skimmer over a flap-type weir. Empty the strainer basket when necessary. Be sure to position the skimmer in the pond where the water is flowing towards it so that the surface debris is carried into the mouth. For example, if you have a waterfall at one end, install the skimmer at the opposite end.

Aeration systems

Some way of introducing air into a koi pond is essential, principally to maintain dissolved oxygen levels to sustain koi metabolism. The main benefit of aeration systems is the churning effect they have on the surface, allowing oxygen to enter the water and carbon dioxide to dissipate. You can introduce air in the following ways.

Using a venturi This simple device fitted in the pumped return pipe underwater draws in air from above the surface and mixes it with the water

Surface skimmer

Left: A surface skimmer in the wall of a koi pond. Fitting a piece of pipework into the mouth of the skimmer will prevent koi becoming trapped as they pursue floating pellets. Make sure that this does not interfere with the normal operation of the skimmer.

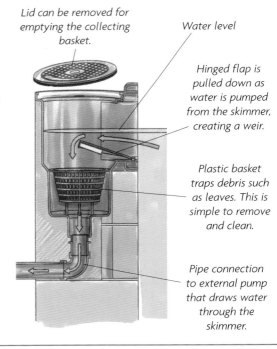

Lid can be removed for emptying the collecting basket.

Water level

Hinged flap is pulled down as water is pumped from the skimmer, creating a weir.

Plastic basket traps debris such as leaves. This is simple to remove and clean.

Pipe connection to external pump that draws water through the skimmer.

passing through to create millions of tiny bubbles. Venturis need a strong water pressure to work efficiently and are not suitable for all types of pumps. Once a familiar sight in koi ponds, venturis are now proving less popular. One reason for this is that the new low-wattage, low-running-cost pumps do not deliver sufficient the necessary high water pressure. Also, reliable airpumps are now reasonably priced and are a more popular option.

Using an airpump This is the best way to aerate your pond. You can feed the pumped air into the water in two ways, through an aerator dome or via airstones.

An aerator dome is a special type of bottom drain used in gravity-fed ponds. An airline from the pump is fed into the drain and the air is released as a column of rising bubbles from a perforated membrane across the top of the dome. Depending on the type of aerator dome you choose, you will need to decide at the building stage whether to install it because you will need to concrete extra pipework into the base of the pond.

Airstones provide the most flexible way of getting air into the pond. They are available in a range of shapes and sizes, the ceramic ones being particularly good at producing a fine stream of bubbles. The simplest way of using an airstone is to connect it to the airpump with plastic airline and drop it over the side of the pond where you need it. You can also use airstones in filter systems to boost the oxygen levels for aerobic bacteria.

Above: This is the type of airpump used to aerate water in a koi system, either in the pond or in the filter chambers. These pumps need to be robust and powerful to supply a useful number of airstones.

How a venturi works

Pumped water

Air is drawn through a plastic pipe from above the water surface.

Aerated water enters the pond.

Restricter speeds up water flow, which reduces pressure and pulls in air.

Water and air colliding with this internal obstruction create a mass of bubbles.

Ozone systems and protein skimmers

Ozone unit

Connection to carbon filter to remove excess ozone and prevent it being released into the air.

Inlet for ozone mixing with incoming water.

Valve to control water flow.

UV unit burns off excess ozone in water.

Gravity return to pond.

Probe from redox meter inserted here measures ozone levels in the water and controls dosing rate.

Water pumped in from last filter chamber.

Ozone generator

Discharge to waste

Ozone gas reacts with pond water in this chamber.

Using ozone is an accepted and familiar technique in the aquarium hobby – particularly in tropical marine fish tanks – but its use in koi ponds is a relatively new application. Ozone (O_3) is an unstable form of oxygen (O_2) and is generated by passing air through a high-voltage electrical discharge. The extra atom of oxygen attached to each molecule easily detaches and in the process has a powerful disinfectant effect, killing any living organisms or cells in the water close by. Clearly, it is also dangerous to the koi and it is vital that no ozone reaches the pond itself.

Pond water is pumped into the ozone unit, either by the main pump or a separate one, and the flow rate through it depends on the pond volume and the size of the unit. Once treated, the water returns to the pond by gravity.

An ozone unit has a marked beneficial effect on koi welfare because it is effectively a self-contained water treatment plant. It will reduce levels of harmful bacteria and parasites, improve water clarity and reduce health problems in the long term. Unfortunately, ozone systems are very expensive and thus out of the reach of many koi-keepers. They can be added later and so are worth considering if your budget allows.

Protein skimmers

Protein skimmers are not essential items but they do provide a way of reducing surface foam and improving water clarity. They make use of the natural tendency for organic molecules to stick to the surface of bubbles. The organic molecules in a koi pond are the fatty and protein waste materials produced by the fish. (The same process is at work in a washing machine as the 'dirt' is 'lifted' off the

Protein skimmer

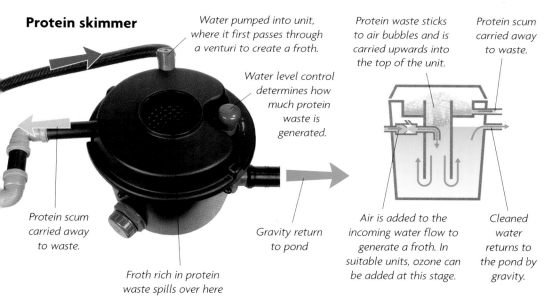

Water pumped into unit, where it first passes through a venturi to create a froth.

Protein waste sticks to air bubbles and is carried upwards into the top of the unit.

Protein scum carried away to waste.

Water level control determines how much protein waste is generated.

Protein scum carried away to waste.

Gravity return to pond

Air is added to the incoming water flow to generate a froth. In suitable units, ozone can be added at this stage.

Cleaned water returns to the pond by gravity.

Froth rich in protein waste spills over here and collects as yellowish liquid in rim.

Below: *Oily surface and long-persisting bubbles are signs of protein waste building up in the pond. Fitting a protein skimmer can solve the problem.*

clothes into the cleansing foam.) The bubbles are created in a protein skimmer by pumping the incoming water through a venturi (see page 25) and keeping them in contact with the water for as long as possible before it returns to the pond by gravity. The air bubbles become coated in protein waste and rise to a collecting cup at the top of the unit. As the bubbles burst, they release the waste and the yellow liquid that builds up can be drained off and discarded. To combine the cleaning and disinfectant process, ozone can be introduced into the airflow at the venturi stage.

Fluidised bed and bubble bead filters

Fluidised bed filters offer the benefits of biological filtration in a very compact unit. Pond water is pumped into a chamber containing a small quantity of special silica sand. The sand swirls up into a constantly moving suspension and the beneficial bacteria that thrive on the surface of the grains cleanse the water of biological wastes. As with ozone units and protein skimmers, the treated water returns to the pond by gravity.

Bubble bead filters

These filters use a medium consisting of small (3x5mm) floating plastic beads. In normal running, the beads float in the upper part of the device, forming a filter bed that carries out biological filtration as well as straining out solid particles down to 15 microns (millionths of a metre) in size – by comparison, a fine sand particle is 50 microns.

Several models are available, depending on the

Fluidised bed filter

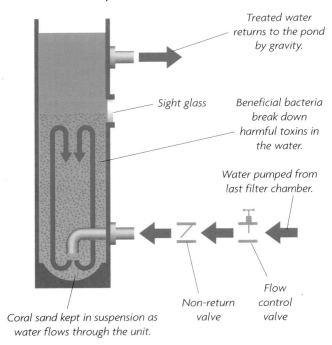

Treated water returns to the pond by gravity.

Sight glass

Beneficial bacteria break down harmful toxins in the water.

Water pumped from last filter chamber.

Coral sand kept in suspension as water flows through the unit.

Non-return valve

Flow control valve

Sand filters

The traditional way of producing 'crystal clear' water in the pond (so-called 'water polishing') has been to install a sand filter after the last main filter stage and just before the water returns to the pond. Sand filters – typically used in swimming pool treatment plants – need a high-pressure, power-hungry pump to force water through fine sand in a sealed container. They provide no biological filtration effect but certainly improve water clarity, albeit with a high-maintenance tariff. Sand filters for koi pond use are being superseded by technically less demanding and more cost-effective water polishing units (see page 30).

Bubble bead filter

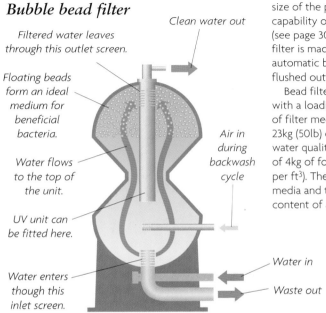

Filtered water leaves through this outlet screen.

Clean water out

Floating beads form an ideal medium for beneficial bacteria.

Water flows to the top of the unit.

UV unit can be fitted here.

Air in during backwash cycle

Water enters though this inlet screen.

Water in

Waste out

size of the pond being treated. All have the capability of being fitted with an integral UV unit (see page 30-31) to control green water. Cleaning the filter is made easy by a valve system that enables automatic backwashing, with collected wastes being flushed out on a regular basis.

Bead filters can maintain acceptable water quality with a loading of up to 8kg of food per day per m^3 of filter media (0.5lb per ft^3). This is equivalent to 23kg (50lb) of koi feeding at a 1% rate. For maximum water quality, this figure is halved to an upper limit of 4kg of food per day per m^3 of bead media (0.25lb per ft^3). These figures are based on standard bead media and typical pelleted foods with a protein content of around 35%.

Below: Clear water allows you to enjoy the full impact of the colours and patterns of your koi. A combination of efficient biological filtration and 'water polishing' will achieve this.

UV clarifiers and mechanical screen filters

Although not essential, a UV clarifier will help to keep the water clear by specifically controlling green water – a suspension of single-celled algae boosted by sunlight and high levels of fertilisers such as nitrates and phosphates. Inside the unit a fluorescent tube radiates ultraviolet (UV) light at the short wavelength end of the purple region of the visible spectrum. UV light is harmful to living tissue and at the right concentration will disrupt the cell contents of the algae, causing them to collapse and decay.

It is important here to make a distinction between a UV clarifier used on a pond and a UV steriliser more commonly used in the tropical freshwater and marine aquarium hobbies. The clarifier allows a relatively large volume of water to pass over the UV light, whereas a steriliser allows a small volume of water to flow close to the light so that it receives a higher 'dose'. This means that a clarifier will affect just the green algae cells, while a steriliser – which has a higher light output as well – is designed to control some bacteria and parasites in the water.

Mechanical screen and sieve filters

These take many forms, but generally contain a screen or sieve that traps very small particles. Although they do not need the high-pressure pump used for a sand filter, some do require a certain amount of pressure to work efficiently. Regular cleaning of the screen or sieve is paramount, particularly when first installed. The following devices use a screening process.

Plastic fin filters consist of a reinforced plastic cylinder with ridged plastic rings acting as the filter medium. The filter body is fitted with a quick-release, snap-type, metal fitting around the lid, which is simple to remove and does not require unions or special pipework. When the cartridge is removed, it can be washed with a hose and reinstated within minutes.

Sieve filters are based on a simple stainless steel box housing a fine sieve that physically strains out solids. The sieve consists of hundreds of laser-cut stainless steel blades arranged in rows at 90° to the water flow, and with aperture options of 50, 100, 150 or 200 microns (millionths of a metre). Water flows through but fine particles – including weed cells,

Sieve filter

Water cascades over weir and through sloping sieve of sharp-edged blades.

Gravity feed from pond

Flap valve with float regulates inflow.

Pump carries away cleaned water.

Solids trapped by stainless steel blades are washed down to the base of the sieve.

UV clarifier

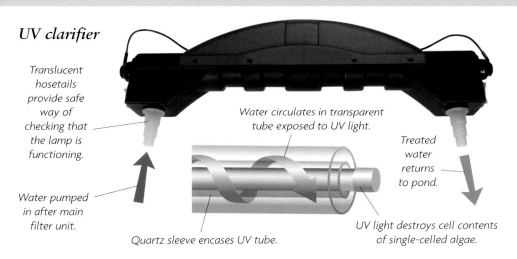

Translucent hosetails provide safe way of checking that the lamp is functioning.

Water pumped in after main filter unit.

Water circulates in transparent tube exposed to UV light.

Treated water returns to pond.

Quartz sleeve encases UV tube.

UV light destroys cell contents of single-celled algae.

fish parasites and their eggs – are trapped.

Pond water is pumped or drawn by gravity over a weir in the body of the device. As it strikes the sharp edges of the blades, surface tension is broken. Dirt particles, or strands of blanketweed, are pushed away from the sieve because of the hydrostatic load created, and because the sieve fits into the body of the unit in a curved profile, the particles end up trapped at the lowest point.

Cylindrical mechanical strainers can be fitted earlier in the 'filtration chain' to the exit pipe from the prefilter or vortex on a gravity system. They consist of a cylindrical device with a stainless steel mesh around the perimeter that prevents solids larger than 100 microns passing through. The screen is constantly cleaned by a water pump that drives a rotor with two revolving spraybars.

Cylindrical mechanical strainer

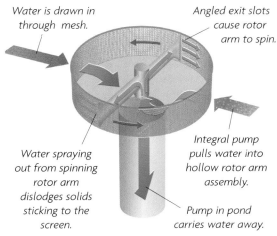

Water is drawn in through mesh.

Angled exit slots cause rotor arm to spin.

Water spraying out from spinning rotor arm dislodges solids sticking to the screen.

Integral pump pulls water into hollow rotor arm assembly.

Pump in pond carries water away.

Trickle towers, vegetable filters and blanketweed control

After the final biological filter stage, treated water can be returned to the pond via a trickle tower to reduce nitrate levels. The plastic media inside the tower – literally a vertical tube down which the water cascades – promote the growth of anaerobic bacteria that strip nitrate (NO_3) of its oxygen atoms to produce nitrogen gas (N_2). Some trickle towers have a revolving spraybar at the top; others have a perforated plate through which the water is sprayed.

Vegetable filters

Vegetable filters are becoming increasingly popular as a means of reducing the nitrate level in the pond and thus helping to control the blanketweed problem (see below). All plant life readily absorbs nitrate and naturally removes it from the water, thus reducing the growth of blanketweed at the end of the nitrogen cycle. However, the vegetable filter has to be large enough to deal with the nitrate that the filter is producing and to date there are no figures available to indicate the pond-to-filter-to-vegetable filter surface area ratio that is required for maximum efficiency. Generally speaking, it would seem that an effective vegetable filter needs to be equivalent to 25% of the surface area of the pond.

Electronic blanketweed devices

Strands of green algae – known as blanketweed – that commonly grow in all kinds of ponds not only look unsightly and cause lowered oxygen levels in summer, but also clog filters, drains, pumps and pipework. Various strategies exist to discourage and clear blanketweed, including chemicals, barley straw and electronic devices that disrupt the algal cells by pulsing magnetic and radio waves through them.

Electronic units are easy to install and seem to have the greatest deterrent effect when added to a new pond that has never suffered blanketweed problems.

Trickle tower

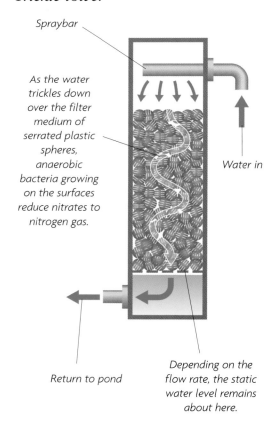

Spraybar

As the water trickles down over the filter medium of serrated plastic spheres, anaerobic bacteria growing on the surfaces reduce nitrates to nitrogen gas.

Water in

Return to pond

Depending on the flow rate, the static water level remains about here.

Electronic blanketweed controller

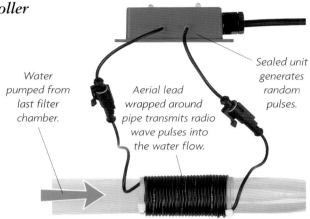

Water pumped from last filter chamber.

Aerial lead wrapped around pipe transmits radio wave pulses into the water flow.

Sealed unit generates random pulses.

Above: A water sample from a pond affected by an algal bloom will look like this – a suspension of algal cells.

A vegetable filter

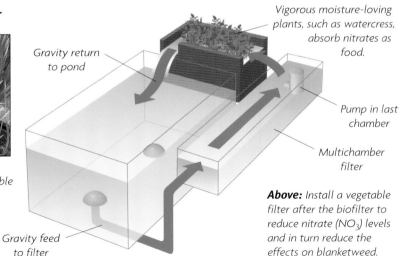

Gravity return to pond

Vigorous moisture-loving plants, such as watercress, absorb nitrates as food.

Pump in last chamber

Multichamber filter

Gravity feed to filter

Above: A simple vegetable filter consisting of a 'runway' with aquatic plants that absorb nitrates (NO₃) given off by the biofilter.

Above: Install a vegetable filter after the biofilter to reduce nitrate (NO₃) levels and in turn reduce the effects on blanketweed.

PART TWO

Building a koi pond

In this section, we look at the two most popular methods of making a koi pond: using a liner or constructing a block-built shell that is then rendered and fibreglassed. We examine each method, from the initial excavation right through to filling and adding the finishing touches to the pond, such as laying decking and edging.

Although the ideal method of construction is to block-build and fibreglass, this is not always the best strategy or possible. If that is the case, it is better to acknowledge it early on and opt for an alternative construction method that suits your needs and ability. Building a koi pond can be technically demanding and it is important that it is done correctly, as the finished pond will be under a lot of stress from the water pressure.

This section is not intended to instruct you in building techniques; rather, it is designed to illustrate and explain each stage involved in the construction process. Unless you are comfortable about laying concrete,

building walls, rendering, etc., it is best to seek professional help and advice. This can take one of two forms. The first is to employ a specialist pond building company to build the whole pond. Alternatively, if you understand the principles involved, you can employ skilled tradespeople to carry out each task. If you opt for this method, it means, in effect, that you become the foreman for the project.

So read this part of the book and if the prospect of building the pond yourself leaves you feeling daunted by the whole idea, the best course is probably to bring in the professionals. Even if you are confident that you can carry out the work yourself, it is still a good idea to run through your plans with your local koi dealer to make sure they are feasible. No matter how well planned the building work may be, there is always one detail that is overlooked and it is far better to have any potential problems pointed out at an early stage than to discover them halfway through the project when it is too late to put them right.

What style of koi pond?

There are some vital differences between a 'garden pond' and a 'koi pond'. It is important to understand these distinctions before we look more closely at how to build a koi pond.

What is a garden pond?

A garden pond is a water feature that enhances the appearance of a garden and supports a wide range of plants and wildlife. A host of aquatic plants can soften the edges of the construction and provide year-round colour and interest, and into this 'jungle' of plants and water, you can introduce goldfish and other hardy pond fish. And the added bonus is that you can create this diverse and successful habitat without worrying too much about a minimum overall size or water depth, and without too much in the way of complicated life-support systems.

Yes, you will need a filter and a water pump if you want to sustain quite a few fish or build a waterfall and fountain, but to a large extent a well set up garden pond is a self-sustaining system.

What is a koi pond?

Like a garden pond, a koi pond is also a hole in the ground filled with water, but there the resemblance ends. A koi pond has a single purpose: to provide a suitable environment for keeping koi. And because koi are fast-growing fish that produce a great deal of waste, the main aim is to create and maintain a large volume of clean, well-oxygenated water in which they can flourish and show off their colours. A koi pond should be at least 1.5m (4ft) deep and must have a filter system that can cope with the heavy demands the koi will put upon it. Unfortunately, since koi will disrupt any plants in the pond, the 'clean functionality' of a koi pond cannot be softened by the addition of aquatic plants, unless they are grown in protected zones.

Of course, this does not mean that a koi pond should not please the eye and become an attractive garden feature, but it will generally take up more space than a garden pond and require more services and equipment, such as the filter system, water supply, drainage pipework, electricity supply for pumps, heaters and water treatment devices, and generally be more 'complicated' and functional.

Left: *Although surrounded by planting, the water of this koi pond is clear of aquatic plants. The water is filtered to a higher standard than in a garden pond in order to cope with the large amounts of waste produced by the fish.*

Above: A well-planted garden pond in midsummer, with the water lilies in flower and the goldfish active and hungry. A garden pond can support a wide range of plants that would not survive the attentions of koi.

Left: An echo of Japan – the home of koi – is commonly seen in Western koi ponds. This wooden bridge and pagoda add an oriental flavour to an informal koi pond photographed in spring.

Choosing the location for your pond

Once you have decided to build a koi pond, the next most important decision is where to put it. Besides purely aesthetic considerations, there are a number of other factors that will influence your choice of location. Here we consider them in turn.

What lies beneath?

Building a koi pond involves a major excavation of the soil in your garden. Be sure to check what lies beneath the surface before you start digging. The main 'obstacles' will be the water supply and gas pipework, electricity cables, rainwater soakaways, manholes and tree roots. You may need to look at your original building plans or consult local utility companies for advice on the location of services to your property.

Connections to utilities

Having discovered where the water, gas and electricity supplies run in your garden, you also need to make sure the pond is conveniently located for connection to them. A koi pond will need a water supply for filling and topping up, a drainage system for carrying away waste water, an electricity supply

Above: *This koi pond at the bottom of this garden is easily viewed through patio windows from the house, which is set at a higher level.*

***Below:** An indoor pond offers many benefits, including easy access and total environmental control. This stylish 36,000-litre (8,000-gallon) pond is heated by a gas boiler.*

to power pumps and other essential equipment, and possibly a gas supply if you plan to include a gas-fired water heating system. If your first choice of location makes it difficult to install these essential services, then think again. It may be better to choose a compromise location to avoid having to dig up that newly laid patio, simply to provide power. And always think ahead; you may wish to upgrade your system in the future and you should establish that electricity cables, for example, will be able to carry a higher load if you install more pumps or additional water treatment devices.

Gaining access to the site

Even a relatively small koi pond entails the shifting of a great deal of soil. Unless you enjoy the back-breaking process of digging the cavity out by hand, you will want to use a mechanical excavator for this fundamental task. Check that your site allows access for such a machine and that you have space to remove any excavated soil that you are not keeping to make a rockery or waterfall feature in the garden. You may need to remove some fence panels during the building process to improve access. If you are not confident about using a mechanical digger, you can hire one complete with an operator to carry out the main excavation work. Although relatively expensive, this will be money well spent to get the project underway.

Position in the garden

Of course, the main point in building a koi pond is so that you can enjoy it. Therefore, choose a location that allows you to view the fish easily on a day-to-day basis. And you will need to provide easy

Above: *Narrow access points to your garden can cause serious problems during the pond building process. Small excavators such as this are the ideal solution for restricted sites.*

access for routine maintenance, even during the cold, wet days of winter. So avoid building the pond in that remote corner of the garden that you rarely use; otherwise you will remember why you never use it! Also consider the position of established trees in the garden. These and other plants may shed leaves into the water that will block up surface skimmers during the autumn and winter. Left in the water, they will rot down and cause pollution problems for the fish. Where suitable, place the pond reasonably close to the house so that you can watch the fish from your window on colder days. But if you do this, take care not to undermine the foundations of the house or any nearby buildings.

39

What type of pond construction?

Depending on your preference and your budget, you can build a koi pond in two main ways: lining the cavity with a flexible sheet of specially formulated plastic or rubber material or building up the walls of the pond from concrete blocks on a concrete foundation slab and then lining this with a flexible liner, painting it with a pond sealant or bonding sheets of fibreglass matting onto the walls with an adhesive resin. Here we consider these options in more detail.

A simple liner pond

Lining the excavation with pond liner is the simplest approach. This method is quick, easy, relatively cheap and suitable for informal shapes (although you may need to sort out the overlaps and creases carefully to avoid creating pockets where debris could be trapped). The main disadvantage is that you must take extra care when cutting and sealing holes in the liner for exit and entry points of pipework associated with drains and pumped water returns. Before installing a liner, be sure to cover the surface of the excavation with a polyester underlay to cushion and protect the liner from any stones or sharp fragments in the soil. You can buy liners in various formulations and thicknesses. Buy one with a lifetime guarantee and source it from a reputable dealer who will honour the warranty.

If you are planning to build a simple liner pond, consider constructing a concrete collar in the shape of the pond before you start digging. It will stabilise the edge of the cavity as you dig down and also forms a firm foundation for the edging stones or slabs around the finished pond. (See pages 44-53 for a step-by-step guide to building a liner pond.)

Above: *This deep pond under construction has been rendered and will be fibreglassed. There are four bottom drains (two in view) in dished zones that aid drainage. The pumped returns are angled for good water circulation within the finished pond.*

A concrete block-built pond

The first step in this construction method involves laying down a slab of concrete as a base, usually with reinforcing steel mesh embedded within it. The walls of the pond are built up using standard 45x23cm (18x9in) pierced concrete blocks, also with steel reinforcement in the form of steel rods passing vertically through the cavities of the blocks. The inside surface of the block wall is then coated with a cement render. To increase the overall strength of the construction, add strands of fibreglass to the render before applying it to the walls. This so-called fibremix can increase the strength of the render by ten times. For a smooth finish, ideally, burn off any protruding strands of fibreglass as the render dries.

Lining or sealing a block-built pond

Once the block shell is complete – and even without rendering the surface – you can line the cavity with a pond liner. Not only does the rigid shell make it easier to fit pipework to the flexible lining material but it also allows the use of box-welded liners that exactly fit the construction without unsightly creases.

An alternative and simple way of finishing the surface of a rendered block-built pond is to paint it with three or four coats of sealant, available in various colours. If you want to achieve the best possible result, seal the surface with sheets of fibreglass matting. This method is relatively expensive – although becoming cheaper – but it does create a tough pond lining that will last for many years. It is not a technique suitable for beginners, or indeed for most koi hobbyists, and so it is best to engage a professional company to carry out the work. Most koi dealers will have a fibreglasser inhouse or be able to engage the services of a specialist team.

Above: This impressive liner pond of 34,000 litres (7,500 gallons) has one bottom drain linked to a gravity-fed filter system consisting of a vortex and a three-chambered filter.

Left: This koi pond is constructed of pierced concrete blocks, which have been rendered and then fibreglassed to create a smooth and durable surface. The pond has a capacity of 25,000 litres (5,600 gallons) and is home to a superb selection of koi.

Pump-fed or gravity-fed pond?

Before making any decisions about filter systems (see pages 10-33), you must decide how to get the water from the pond to a filter and back again. You have two choices: a pump-fed system or a gravity-fed system. Both have their advantages, but for a koi pond a gravity-fed setup is the one to choose.

Pump-fed filter systems

In this system, dirty water is pumped from the pond to an external filter and 'clean' water returns to the pond by gravity. One disadvantage of this system is that because the pump is in the pond, it is liable to become blocked and needs frequent cleaning. The second main problem with a pump-fed system is that the external filter must be higher than the water level in the pond so that clean water can flow back under gravity. This not only means that the returning water has little or no pressure (to power venturis, for example) but also the pump needs to be powerful enough to lift the water up into the filter system.

An external filter can be unsightly and difficult to disguise. The pipework carrying water from the filter

back to the pond must be level or sloping towards the pond. As this water is at a very low pressure, you will need a large-bore pipe to prevent the filter filling up quicker than it can empty. This return pipe can also be a difficult feature to hide.

Although a pump-fed filter is relatively cheap and easy to install, you will never be able to pump all the waste from the bottom of the pond and will need a vacuum cleaning device to do this effectively. Ease of construction and installation is a trade-off against the increased amount and expense of maintenance once the system is up and running.

Gravity-fed filter systems

In a gravity-fed filter system the water in the filter is at the same level as that in the pond. A wide-bore pipe drains water from the bottom of the pond into the filter. This means that the filter can be buried next to the pond, or if the pond is raised, the filter is also raised by the same amount. In ponds up to 18,000 litres (4,000 gallons) capacity, a single drain in the centre of the pond base will be sufficient.

Left: This large, gravity-fed pond supports a good collection of koi that are completely at home in their mature garden setting. The filter system runs alongside the pond under decking.

In larger ponds, two or more drains will be needed. Once the pond is filled with water it will flow into and also fill the filter system. To set up a circulation, a submersible pump is placed in the final filter chamber or an external pump is fitted in the pipework after the filter system. The pump propels cleaned water back into the pond and dirty water from the pond base flows into the filter by gravity to take its place. Because the pump handles filtered water, it is unlikely to clog and needs very little maintenance. Also, it is easy to reach the pump for maintenance, repair or replacement. Because the water is pumped back to the pond, the return pipes can be relatively small (42-50mm/1.5-2.0in diameter is normal) and these can be positioned below water level, resulting in no visible pipework.

Pump-fed pond

Filtered water flows back to the pond under gravity, usually via a waterfall or stream.

A submersible pump draws water from the pond.

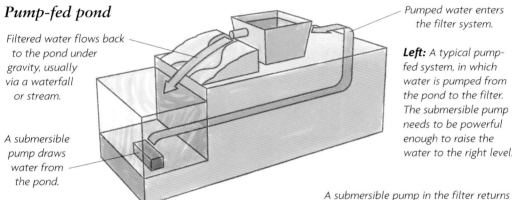

Pumped water enters the filter system.

Left: A typical pump-fed system, in which water is pumped from the pond to the filter. The submersible pump needs to be powerful enough to raise the water to the right level.

Gravity-fed pond

Right: This is a typical gravity-fed system, in which the filter is at the same level as the pond and the water flows into the filter by gravity. A pump in the filter returns water to the pond.

The water level in the pond and the filter are the same.

A submersible pump in the filter returns water to the pond, thereby starting up the flow from the pond.

Water flows to the filter by gravity through a drain at the bottom of the pond.

Liner pond – estimating the size

A liner pond is by far the easiest form of pond to install and suitable not only as a garden pond but also, despite popular belief, for koi. A liner pond is thought to be inappropriate for koi because if it is to include a gravity-fed filtration system, it means making holes in the liner for drains and returns, thereby risking leakages. However, it is not difficult to install these pieces of equipment, although you must take extra care when carrying out the work. If you follow the steps outlined here, you should have no problem setting up a well-functioning, watertight, gravity-fed pond using a liner.

Many people find the prospect of installing a liner pond less daunting than building a block-built one because the construction process simply involves digging a hole and putting in the liner. This is certainly true, although obviously adding a gravity-fed filter system requires a certain amount of extra construction to ensure that the drains do not move about. This normally means encasing the pipework in a channel of concrete. There is no need to construct a solid base or 23cm (9in) block walls up from the base, as the overall strength of the pond is provided by the liner and the soil behind it. The only other construction work involves laying a concrete collar around the top of the pond for support, plus any brickwork if the pond is to be raised above ground level.

What you will need

Concrete	Underlay
Ballast	Cold glue tape
Sand	Edging slabs or rocks
110mm (4in) bottom drain	Digger or shovel
110mm (4in) pipe for drain	Skips or grabber lorries to remove waste
38 or 50mm (1.5-2in) pipe for return pipework	Insurance for any machinery on site, such as diggers or hired tools
Filter	
Pump	Blocks if the pond is to be built above ground
UV clarifier	
Liner	Mortar for blocks

Raised ponds

If you are planning to raise a liner pond out of the ground, build the walls using 23cm (9in) reinforced hollow concrete blocks. Tie these to the concrete collar around the rim of the pond using reinforced steel rods. You can then face them with brickwork, as shown in this pond.

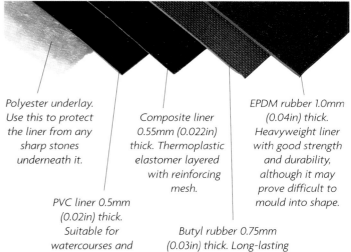

Polyester underlay. Use this to protect the liner from any sharp stones underneath it.

Composite liner 0.55mm (0.022in) thick. Thermoplastic elastomer layered with reinforcing mesh.

EPDM rubber 1.0mm (0.04in) thick. Heavyweight liner with good strength and durability, although it may prove difficult to mould into shape.

PVC liner 0.5mm (0.02in) thick. Suitable for watercourses and small ponds.

Butyl rubber 0.75mm (0.03in) thick. Long-lasting liner that can be welded.

Above: A liner pond is literally a hole in the ground lined with a rubber or plastic sheet to stop the water draining away. The most important thing is to make sure the liner is big enough.

Working out the size of the liner

To work out the size of the liner you need for your pond, first measure the length, width and depth of your excavation. Then double the depth measurement and add this figure to both the length and the width measurements. You will also need to allow for an overlap around the edge so that you can anchor and conceal the liner with stones, bricks or slabs. Adding 60cm (24in) to the adjusted length and width measurements will give you a 30cm (12in) overlap around the perimeter.

Overlap margin of 30cm (12in) around the edge.

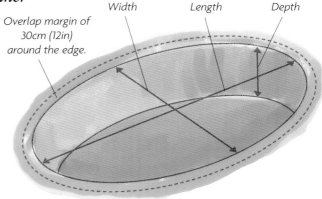

Width   Length   Depth

Liner pond – making a concrete collar

To create a firm and even foundation for the liner and edging stones and to prevent the soil collapsing as you dig the hole, first build a concrete collar (also called a ring beam) around the pond edge. Plan where the returns and pipework are to go and incorporate them into the collar.

Once the concrete collar has set, begin digging out the pond. If you are opting for a gravity-fed system, try to dig out a slight gradient running from the outside walls to the centre or to the point where you intend placing the bottom drain. Also dig out the site for the filter, allowing for the fact that when the excavation is complete, the top of the filter should be about 2.5cm (1in) above the water level in the pond.

If you are installing a bottom drain, now is the time to dig the trench for the pipework.

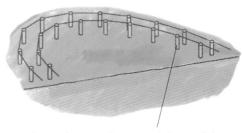

Start by marking out the internal shape of the pond with pegs and string. When you are happy with the shape, set out a second series of pegs 23cm (9in) away from the first, mirroring the internal shape.

Be sure to position surface skimmers and pipework before pouring concrete into the trench.

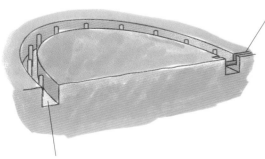

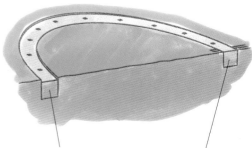

Dig out a trench 23cm (9in) deep between the two series of pegs. If the ground is uneven, remove the two sets of marker pegs and reposition them vertically along the centre of the trench. Check that the tops of the pegs are level all the way round and adjust any that are not.

Once you have laid in any return pipework, etc., pour the concrete into the trench up to the top of each peg. Leave the pegs in place.

The concrete collar will provide a level base for the edging stones and will be disguised by them.

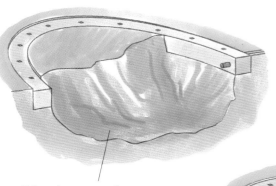

Right: A 110mm (4in) bottom drain with a flange that fits on top of the pond liner and holds it in place to create a watertight seal. The domed cover, fitted at a later stage, will prevent fish swimming into the drain.

Drain casing

When the concrete has set, you can safely excavate the soil inside the collar. Make the base as flat as possible so that the liner will fit smoothly later on.

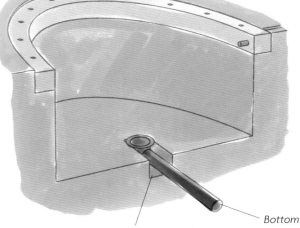

Above: If you are digging out the cavity with a spade, try not to stand on the collar as you dig and do not use it as a lever for the spade, otherwise the edge will break.

Mark out the position of the bottom drain and 110mm (4in) pipe run. These must be totally encased in concrete, so dig a trench in the base of the excavation about 38cm (15in) deep. Fill the trench with about 15cm (6in) of concrete to support the drain and pipe run and allow it to set.

Bottom drain and pipework in position, ready to be encased in concrete.

Liner pond – installing the liner

The pipe from the drain will run to the edge of the pond, where it will be extended up to ground level ready to be cut down for connection to the filter system. Both the horizontal and vertical pipe run will need to be encased in concrete to support them from the water pressure once the pond is filled.

When all the concrete has set, line the pond with underlay in preparation for the liner. A layer of sand beneath the underlay will provide extra protection. Cut holes in the underlay around the bottom drains and any inlet pipe. Make absolutely sure that no underlay runs over any flanges that will be sealed to the liner at a later stage, otherwise it may not be possible to achieve a watertight seal. Now place the liner into position, ready for sealing onto the bottom drain. Before cutting any holes, push the liner firmly into all the corners, so that it cannot move once it is sealed. If you wish, you can fill the pond with a small amount of water to ensure that the liner is secure. Then pump away the water and leave the liner to dry.

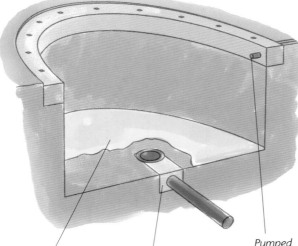

Lay a 5cm (2in) layer of sand over the base to cushion the underlay and liner.

Place the drain and pipework on top of the set concrete layer in the trench and encase them in concrete. Do not attach the domed cover of the bottom drain at this stage.

Pumped return pipe protruding through concrete collar.

> ### Box welding for liner ponds
>
> You can order a liner made to fit your pond exactly, with no folds or creases. Your koi dealer will weld panels of liner together to match the excavation. This works best for formal-shaped ponds, such as circular, rectangular or square.

Above: Before installing the underlay, sweep the concrete collar free of stones. Also remove any stones in the hole and prise out roots from nearby trees.

Above: Spun underlays are by far the best, as they allow water to move through them. This prevents water from being trapped between the liner and underlay and stops roots penetrating the liner. Buy plenty so that you have some spare for a waterfall.

Above: When you get your pond liner home, check it carefully for tears and imperfections; once you have installed it, you will not be able to remove it. Replace the liner in its packaging and store it in a safe place until you are ready to use it.

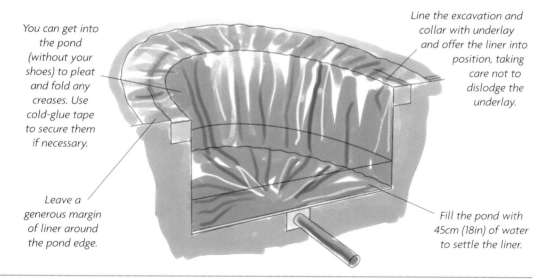

You can get into the pond (without your shoes) to pleat and fold any creases. Use cold-glue tape to secure them if necessary.

Leave a generous margin of liner around the pond edge.

Line the excavation and collar with underlay and offer the liner into position, taking care not to dislodge the underlay.

Fill the pond with 45cm (18in) of water to settle the liner.

Liner pond – installing the bottom drain

When you are satisfied that the liner is in place, locate the top flanges for the drain and other pipework in the correct position and secure them with a suitable sealant and the screws supplied with the fittings. Only now should you begin to make any incisions into the liner. When cutting holes it is best to work from the centre outwards, using the secured fittings as your cutting guide. If the holes are cut before the fittings are in position, it may prove impossible to match them up!

Before fitting the tank connector, secure it to the liner (i.e. on both sides of the liner with the stainless steel screws screwed up) using a suitable sealant. Then cut through the liner to make the hole. If you make the hole before securing the tank connector, the cut edges do not lie flat and it is difficult to get a smooth union. Solvent-weld the tank connector to the return pipe in the wall of the pond.

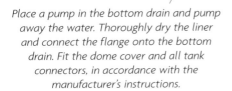

Place a pump in the bottom drain and pump away the water. Thoroughly dry the liner and connect the flange onto the bottom drain. Fit the dome cover and all tank connectors, in accordance with the manufacturer's instructions.

Right: The best way of minimising creases in a pond liner is to use cold glue tape, which is like a heavy duty version of double-sided tape.

Below: Warm the tape first with a hairdryer and stick it to the edge of the fold. Remove the paper backing and push the fold in place. It will be hard to reposition once fixed.

Securing the bottom drain

1 When the liner is fully in place, climb into the pond and locate the drain through the liner. Place the top flange in position and hold it steady as you make a small incision in the liner inside the flange.

2 Take the flange and cover the underside with a suitable sealant ready for sealing in place. Do not hold back on the sealant as this will create the watertight seal.

3 Position the top flange, which is covered in sealant, onto the liner so that it lines up with the base of the drain. Once aligned, tighten the screws to secure the unit.

4 Extend the initial incision in the liner outwards to the now fully secured flange. Trim away the unwanted liner, following the circumference of the flange.

5 The pipe that fits into the drain allows you to set the dome height. Push it into the socket, but do not glue it; you may need to remove it for access later on.

6 With the pipe in place, push the dome cover onto it. Once again, do not glue it in position in case you need to remove it in the future for maintenance.

Liner pond – the finishing touches

Before filling the pond – and while the liner is dry and clean – you may wish to secure any creases in the liner using a product called 'cold glue tape'. To determine where any creases may occur, add a small amount of water to the pond to pull the sides of the liner tight as shown on page 49. Then empty the pond again and let the liner dry out before applying the tape. To finish off the final edging around the pond, use coping stones, rock, bricks or any another suitable material. There are various ways of neatening the edges of the liner, but do not forget that it is creating a waterproof seal and must therefore run under or up whatever edging you choose.

Your liner pond is now complete and all that remains is to install the filters, which must be level with the water in the pond. The installation of the filter system is explained on pages 60-63 for a block-built pond, but the same method applies here. When it is in place and all the pipework is connected, fill the pond and commission the system.

Complete the edge of the pond with slabs, brickwork, slate or stones and fill the pond using a flowmeter.

Use a tank connector to seal the liner to the pipe. Make a watertight seal, using a suitable sealant, as explained on page 50. Cut the return pipe flush with the liner.

__Below:__ A typical water meter, with connections to fit a standard hosepipe. These units do not normally reset to zero, so it is important to note the start reading before using the meter so that you can subtract it from the final reading.

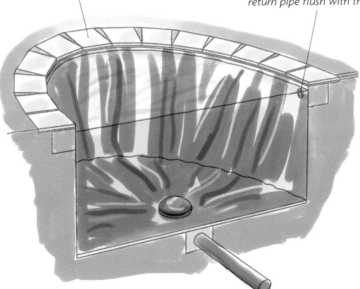

Left: The paving slabs used along the edge of this liner pond have lost their new 'rawness' and have taken on a more mellow, aged appearance. They provide a stable platform for viewing the fish.

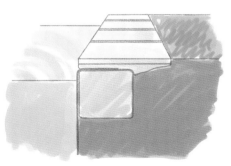

Left: Slabs form a neat and stable edge for a koi pond. The underlay and liner overlap the concrete collar and are covered by paving.

Right: If you place boulders around the edge, support them on a liner offcut to protect the pond liner.

Above: You can conceal the edge of the liner between vertical courses of bricks, as shown here. The concrete collar makes an ideal foundation for the brickwork. If the pond is to be raised by more than a few courses, build it up with blocks and finish the external walls with brick, concealing the liner between the blocks and the brickwork.

Block-built pond – planning and excavation

Here we follow the steps involved in the construction of a partly raised, oval, concrete-rendered koi pond. It will have an estimated capacity of 22,700 litres (5,000 gallons) and be equipped with a vortex filtration system, heating, UV clarifier, aeration and a water purifier.

Start by marking out the area on the ground. This pond will measure approximately 4.5x3m (15x10ft), but an extra 35cm (14in) has been allowed all the way

Left: For informal shapes, lay a brightly coloured hosepipe on the ground and view the results from an upstairs window until you are happy with the result.

round to incorporate a 23cm (9in) block wall, part of which will have a brickwork facing. As the pond is to be 60cm (24in) above ground level, excavate the area to a depth of 135cm (54in) so that the final pond depth will be approximately 1.5m (5ft).

Having completed the pond excavation, set out the area for the filter system. In this instance it will require a floor area of 3.7x2.5m (12x8ft) and will be the same depth as the pond. To determine the exact height needed for the filters, adjust the thickness of the concrete base laid in this area.

This is also a good time to think about the pipework that will return the water to the pond, plus any additional pipework that may be needed for removing waste water. Consider where it will go and, if necessary, excavate the designated areas. If the pond is some distance from utilities such as water and electricity, run a trench for them now, as this may be the only time when an excavator is on site.

How to mark out a shape

Marking out the shape of your new pond on the ground and trying to get an idea of how it will look in your garden are vital first steps in the planning process. The small-scale examples in these photographs demonstrate some simple techniques for marking out circles and ovals. Instead of sand in a bottle, you could use a can of spray chalk.

Right: Using a loop of string running around two pegs spaced apart will give you a perfect oval shape on the ground.

Left: To mark out a circle, position your marker inside a loop of string held taut around a peg at the centre of the space.

Water level in the pond and filter

The water level in the pond determines the height of the filter system. The level must be the same in each for the gravity-fed system to work.

Pond

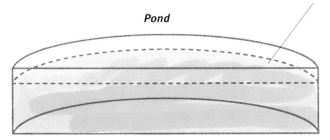

Filter

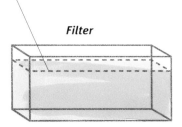

The pond construction

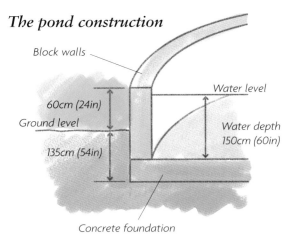

Block walls

60cm (24in)

Ground level

135cm (54in)

Water level

Water depth
150cm (60in)

Concrete foundation

Right: *A mini digger in action. These machines can be hired with or without a driver, and are invaluable if there is access to the site. Remember that while the machine is on hire it is your responsibility, so take out insurance against theft or damage.*

Block-built pond – laying the foundations

Now it is time to construct the base of the pond by pouring in concrete to a final depth of 30-45cm (12-18in). When you have added the first 15-20cm (6-8in) of concrete, allow it to set. Then lay in the 12-18mm (0.5-0.75in)-gauge reinforced steel bars and position the bottom drain, or drains. Add more concrete until you reach the final depth and allow the finished base to set. Do not pour the concrete base into the filter area at this stage, as it is vital that the water level of the pond and that of the vortex system are the same. You will not be able to judge this until the walls of the pond are built.

Right: *An alternative strategy involves laying a matrix of reinforced steel before any concrete is poured. It is raised off the ground with blocks, so that the concrete flows around the steel. The bottom drain (a different design from the one featured elsewhere in this book) is covered to prevent any cement falling into it.*

Installing the bottom drain

Push (never glue) a drain cover into place, leaving a gap of 13-25mm (0.5-1in).

Steel reinforcing mesh

Concrete sub-base

A second layer of concrete encases all the pipework and drains.

The 110mm (4in) pipe to the filter must be as level as possible to avoid waste collecting in any high or low points.

Laying the foundations

The walls of the pond are built onto a concrete base. The thicker the base the better, as each 1,000 litres (220 gallons) of water weighs about 990kg (2,200lb).

A 110mm (4in) pipe runs from the bottom drain to the filter system.

Using an aerated bottom drain

If your pond design incorporates an aerated bottom drain, it may be necessary to run additional pipework in the base of the pond to accommodate the airline that delivers the air to the unit. This type of bottom drain cannot be added at a later stage, so you must decide early in the construction process whether you want to use one in the pond.

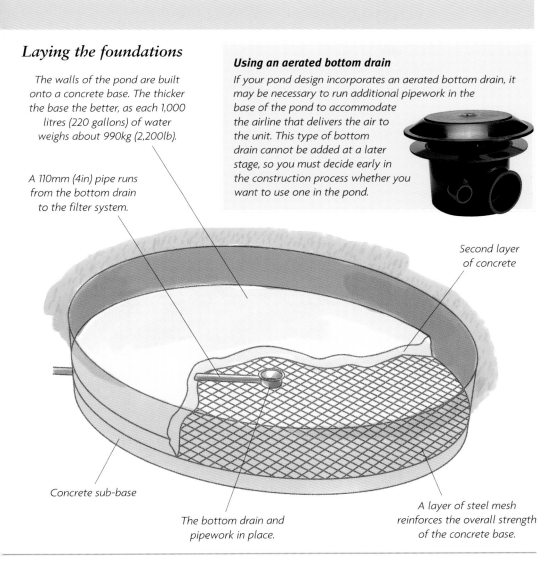

Second layer of concrete

Concrete sub-base

The bottom drain and pipework in place.

A layer of steel mesh reinforces the overall strength of the concrete base.

Block-built pond – building the walls

Build up the pond walls using 23cm (9in) reinforced hollow blocks. These create a honeycomb effect and must be backfilled with concrete. At the same time, insert 16-20mm (0.625-0.8in)-gauge reinforced steel bars. As you build up the blockwork, allow for two water returns leading from the pond to the filter system. One return should be 30-35cm (12-14in) below the water surface and the other 30-35cm (12-14in) up from the base of the pond. These returns should pass through the wall of the pond at an angle of 45°, so that optimum water circulation can be achieved within the pond. This type of return is known as a TPR (Tangential Pond Return). As you complete the last course of blocks, set the surface skimmer at the 'end' of the water's circulation around the pond to ensure that all surface debris is pushed towards the skimmer. Depending on the type of skimmer, the water level may not be at the top of the unit. Position the skimmer so that when the pond is filled, the water is at the correct level. When the pond is the required height, and while you wait for the blockwork to dry, you can install the filter system.

Above: The pond walls are built from 23x45cm (9x18in) hollow blocks. The finish is somewhat untidy, but eventually both sides will be rendered. In our project, the external walls will be hidden by face brickwork.

Adding extra strength

Reinforced steel bars add strength to block walls. The more you use, the stronger the construction. As a guide, use vertical bars at any weak points, such as the corners on a square pond, or at strategic points on a curved or circular pond.

Right: This method of construction uses the highest level of reinforcement, with vertical steel bars placed in all the blocks and horizontal ones laid between each course of blockwork.

Above: Once the walls are built, concrete is poured down the gaps in the block. When set, this creates a solid concrete post joining together all the blocks in that column.

The walls take shape

Water circulates around pond towards the skimmer.

Outlet from skimmer to external pump

Pumped return from filter

Position the surface skimmer in the block wall where the water flow generated by the pumped returns will 'push' floating debris towards it.

Left: Leave space in the wall of the pond for the surface skimmer. You can then position it before concreting it into place. Leave enough pipe on the feed from the skimmer so that you can cut it to the exact length once the skimmer is firmly set in place.

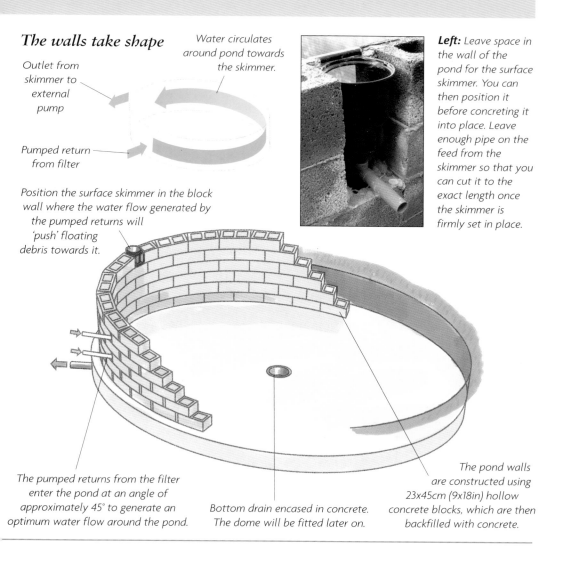

The pumped returns from the filter enter the pond at an angle of approximately 45° to generate an optimum water flow around the pond.

Bottom drain encased in concrete. The dome will be fitted later on.

The pond walls are constructed using 23x45cm (9x18in) hollow concrete blocks, which are then backfilled with concrete.

Block-built pond – installing the filter system

Before you fill the base of the filter with concrete, make sure that the tops of your filters are about 2.5cm (1in) above the intended water level in the pond. Use a laser level to help you arrive at the precise height of the filter system.

This pond system features three vortex chambers installed in a line. Connect vortex 1 to the bottom drain of the pond, with a 110mm (4in) slide valve fitted in line. Connect vortex 1, 2 and 3 using 110mm (4in) pipework and join vortex 3 to the pump using 38mm (1.5in) pipework. Before the pipe enters the pump, fit a T piece to allow the skimmer to be

inserted into the pipe run. Water from the filter will flow into one side of the T piece and water from the skimmer into the other. Connect the 'combined' part of the T to the suction side of the pump. It is advisable to install a ball valve on all sides of the T to allow you to control the amount of water being drawn from the skimmer and filter independently.

On the flow side of the pump, the pipework should run to the UV unit and from there to a gas-fired boiler or electric heater. The flow from the heater will be divided between the two returns already built into the pond wall.

How the filter connects with the pond

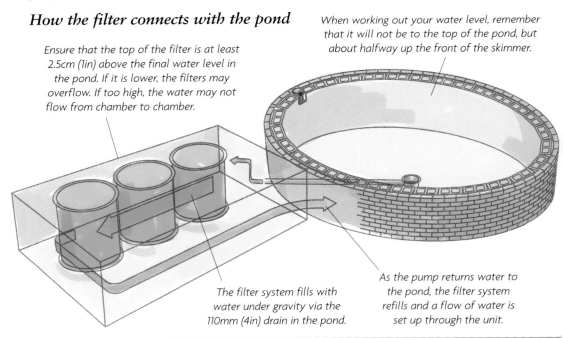

Ensure that the top of the filter is at least 2.5cm (1in) above the final water level in the pond. If it is lower, the filters may overflow. If too high, the water may not flow from chamber to chamber.

When working out your water level, remember that it will not be to the top of the pond, but about halfway up the front of the skimmer.

The filter system fills with water under gravity via the 110mm (4in) drain in the pond.

As the pump returns water to the pond, the filter system refills and a flow of water is set up through the unit.

How the filter system works

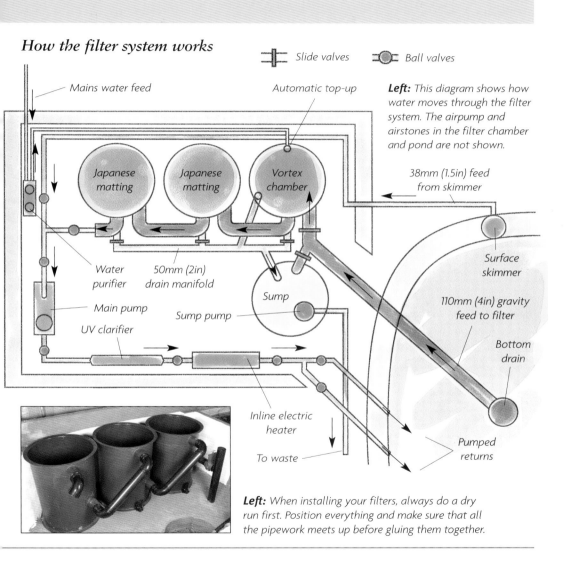

Slide valves   Ball valves

Mains water feed

Automatic top-up

Left: This diagram shows how water moves through the filter system. The airpump and airstones in the filter chamber and pond are not shown.

Japanese matting

Japanese matting

Vortex chamber

38mm (1.5in) feed from skimmer

Surface skimmer

110mm (4in) gravity feed to filter

Bottom drain

Water purifier

50mm (2in) drain manifold

Sump

Main pump

Sump pump

UV clarifier

Inline electric heater

To waste

Pumped returns

Left: When installing your filters, always do a dry run first. Position everything and make sure that all the pipework meets up before gluing them together.

Block-built pond – installing the filter system

To simplify any future maintenance of the filter system, you should fit 38mm (1.5in) ball valves on each side of the UV clarifier, heater, pump, skimmer and the two pond returns. This will enable you to remove and replace each piece of equipment individually.

Finally, fit the airstones from your chosen air system, the water purifying unit and a self-topping ballcock to vortex 1. If you decide to fit an overflow to the system, this should also be connected to vortex 1. Excavate a soakaway so that you can discharge the water from the vortex system for cleaning, and drain it away using a sump pump. The soakaway should be at least 5m (16ft) away from the house.

Below: *The pump receives water from the third vortex chamber and from the surface skimmer and pumps it via the UV clarifier and heater back to the pond.*

This overflow pipe from vortex 1 connects with a manifold of 50mm (2in) pipes connecting all three vortex chambers and carrying waste to the sump via 50mm (2in) slide valves.

These are the 110mm (4in) pipes connecting the three vortex chambers, from the top of one to the bottom of the next.

This is the 110mm (4in) feed from the bottom drain to the first vortex chamber.

This 82mm (3in) pipe and valve enables the bottom drain to be flushed without interfering with the vortex chambers.

Small soakaway 75cm (30in) across and 105cm (42in) deep with a sump pump in the bottom, pumping to the main soakaway.

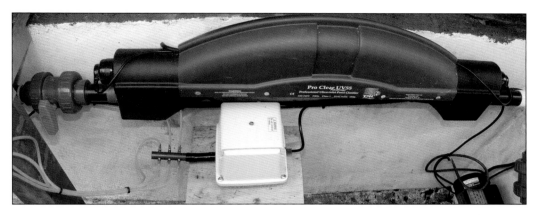

Above: The water purifier is fed with mains water and supplies treated water to the self-topping ballcock in the first vortex.

Above: The UV clarifier installed. A double union ball valve has been fitted before and after the unit, so that the water flow through it can be stopped and the unit removed by undoing one of the unions on each of the valves. The airpump for the pond can also be seen, with the airline running from it to wherever you wish the air to be delivered. In this system the airpump could be located above, or at the same level as the water in the pond. If the pump is located below water level, fit non-return valves to stop any water back siphoning down the airlines in the event of a power cut.

Below: These are the two pump returns to the pond seen from the filter bay side. A ball valve installed on each pipe allows the flow balance between them to be adjusted or each can be shut off. Notice the 45° angle at which the 38mm (1.5in) pipes pass through the pond wall.

Block-built pond – fibreglassing the walls

The best way to provide a waterproof seal is to treat the internal walls of the pond with fibreglass. Render the walls first and shape the floor with render in a neat, even spiral down to the bottom drain. Add fibre mix to the render to strengthen it.

To fibreglass the pond, apply a layer of resin to an area of wall, followed by one sheet of fibreglass matting. Continue round the pond in this way, overlapping the sheets of matting by 5-7.5cm (2-3in). When two sheets have been laid, place an additional sheet overlapping each sheet by a half. Finally, apply a third layer of resin using a paddle roller to stipple and ensure an even spread. It is a good idea to carry out this procedure when the ambient temperature is above 15°C (59°F) so that the resin can cure completely.

Allow the fibreglassing to dry out for 24 hours and then thoroughly rub down the entire area with sandpaper to remove any rough edges and burs. When you are happy with the surface, apply an even layer of coloured top coat. Make sure that the top coat is applied in one continuous process.

1 Coat the rendered pond wall with resin and apply a sheet of chopped strand fibreglass matting.

2 Apply firm and even pressure with a roller impregnated with resin to fix the sheet in place.

3 Make sure that the matting adheres to the curved surfaces, here near the base of the pond.

Right: *A sample of 300gm/m² chopped strand matting. Wear protective gloves and, ideally, a face mask when handling any form of fibreglass and resin.*

4 Use a paddle roller to release any air trapped within the matting. The surface will be getting very sticky at this stage.

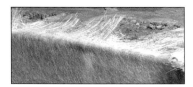

5 It is vital to finish off the edges of the pond cleanly and effectively. Ensure that the top edge around the pond has an overlap margin of 5-7.5cm (2-3in).

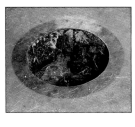

Above: The flange of the bottom drain is clearly visible through the layers of fibreglass matting used on the internal surfaces of this pond.

6 Make sure that the turned-over edge of matting is thoroughly drenched with resin by repeated application of the impregnated roller.

Above: Make sure that plastic skimmers and bottom drains are etched with sandpaper before fibreglassing to ensure a good key.

Left: The surface skimmer after fibreglassing, with all the edges smoothed off.

7 Use the ridged paddle roller to consolidate the edge and ensure that no bubbles are left in the matting.

Right: Apply a top coat to the fibreglassed surface to complete the internal walls of the pond. Make sure that you complete this in one application.

Block-built pond – the finishing touches

Once the pond is finished, wait at least 48 hours before washing it out and discharging the water. This will remove any residues of cement, fibreglass or anything else that may prove hazardous to your fish before you introduce them.

When you fill the pond for the first time, use a water meter so that you can make a note of the exact capacity. This will be important later on if you need to treat the fish with any medication, when accurate dosing is crucial. Although you can buy a water meter, many koi dealers hire them for a small charge, which is ideal for a one-time use.

If you intend to put fish in the pond straightaway, you should add a biofilter startup chemical to the filter system. At this early stage, there will be no beneficial bacteria present in the filter to break down ammonia and the resultant nitrites produced as waste products by the fish. The biofilter startup chemical will speed up the maturation of the filter medium so that it begins to cleanse the water. Ideally, though, it is far better to fill the pond and allow it to run for 48 to 72 hours before introducing any fish, as this will allow the water to reach the ambient or heated temperature, and any excess chlorine will be dispersed. After this period, you can add one or two fish every few days. This avoids overloading the new filter and gives it time to adapt to the increasing waste loads being placed upon it. It is still a good idea to use a biofilter startup, even if you adopt this preferred method. Furthermore, if the water has not passed through a purifier, treat it with a suitable dechlorinator to remove chlorine, chloramine and metals. Add the dose you need to a watering can of pond water and sprinkle it onto the pond surface or into the surface skimmer.

Above: *The block-built pond nearing completion. The filtration systems are housed under wooden decking, with trapdoors to provide easy access.*

Above: *Decking is used over the filters, brick hides the external wall and slate edges the pond. All these materials have been checked to ensure that they are fish safe.*

The completed pond

Do not cover the top of the skimmer with pond edging (or make it removable) because you will need access to empty the collecting basket.

Paving slabs or rocks are generally used to finish the pond edge. It is best to use an impervious material because it will not allow any water to pass through it. If you do use a permeable rock or other material, seal it to reduce the risk of it leaking into the pond. Also seal any cement used to hold down the slabs/rocks around the pond for the same reason.

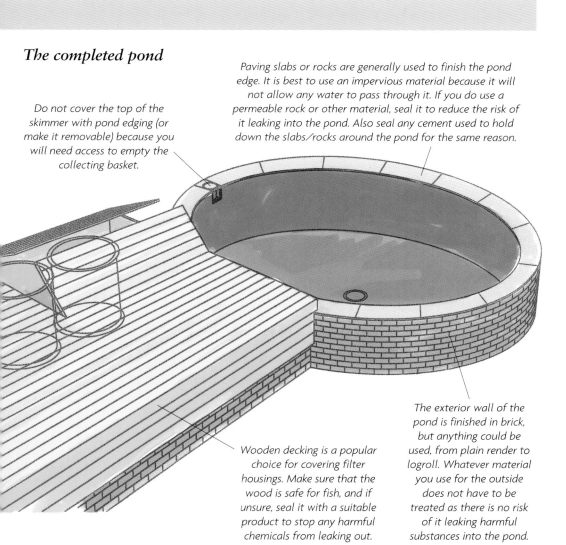

The exterior wall of the pond is finished in brick, but anything could be used, from plain render to logroll. Whatever material you use for the outside does not have to be treated as there is no risk of it leaking harmful substances into the pond.

Wooden decking is a popular choice for covering filter housings. Make sure that the wood is safe for fish, and if unsure, seal it with a suitable product to stop any harmful chemicals from leaking out.

Maintaining a pump-fed system

Here we look at the specific tasks that together make up a maintenance regime that will keep a pump-fed pond in good condition. Following these recommendations will ensure that your pond provides a healthy and stable environment.

Daily

Feed fish The fundamental task for every koi-keeper is to feed the fish – one of the most rewarding aspects of the hobby and not merely a chore.

Check fish Feeding the fish gives you an opportunity to check their general health and behaviour, and spot any potential problems as soon as they develop.

Check appliances Monitoring the equipment that keeps the pond functioning efficiently will alert you to any malfunctions before they have a major effect.

Weekly

Clean the pump In pump-fed systems, the pump is in the pond, where it continuously draws dirty water into the filter system. If the pump has a sponge prefilter, clean this at least once a week. If you are using a pump designed to pump solids, it will not need cleaning so often.

Clean the mechanical filter media Most pump-fed filter systems have a compartment containing a mechanical medium, such as foam or brushes, that will trap suspended solids. The amount of solids entering the filter will depend on the pump you are using – one with a prefilter will pass on less solids than one without. It is important that you only clean out the mechanical stage of your filter on a weekly

basis. At the same time, discharge any waste from the filter if your system has the facility to do this.

Test the water Choose from the many water testing kits available on the market and stick to the same ones for consistent results (see page 96-99).

Monthly

Vacuum clean the pond Waste will collect on the bottom of a pump-fed pond and the best way to remove it is to use a pond vacuum cleaner. Most vacuum devices pump water out of the pond during the cleaning process. This is not a bad thing, because a water change of up to 20% is beneficial. Cleaning the pond regularly will not only reduce the waste, but in the longer term it will actually cut down the time spent vacuuming and the resultant water loss.

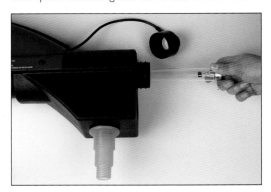

Above: *UV bulbs only last at the strength needed to stop green water for six months. Keep a record of when you change the bulb. Do not touch the glass and avoid damaging the internal quartz sleeve.*

Half-yearly

Change the UV tube If you are using a UV clarifier to control green water, change the UV tube every six months. To be effective, the tube needs to be working at 100% light output and this can normally only be guaranteed in the first six months of its life.

Yearly

Complete system clean out Give your filter system a complete clean out once a year. Stagger the process by cleaning out separate sections of the filter on different weeks. And be sure to use pond water to clean the biological media.

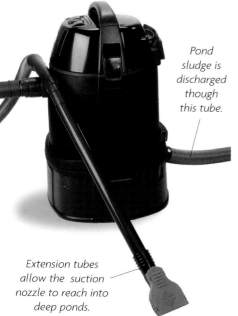

Pond sludge is discharged though this tube.

Extension tubes allow the suction nozzle to reach into deep ponds.

Above: *Pond vacuum cleaners such as this can be used to remove sludge and debris from the pond floor or filter. The waste collects in the unit before being discharged to waste.*

Pump-fed maintenance schedule

	Daily	Weekly	Monthly	Half yearly	Yearly
Feed the fish	●				
Check fish	●				
Check appliances	●				
Clean pump		●			
Clean media		●			
Test water		●			
Vacuum pond			●		
Change UV lamp				●	
Clean out filter system					●

Maintaining a gravity-fed system

Essential maintenance for a gravity-fed pond is the same as for a pump-fed one, plus the extra attention needed for any additional systems, such as surface skimmers, heating, aeration, vortex chambers, etc.

Daily

Feed and check fish, check appliances Follow the general advice on page 68 and refer to the sections on feeding and health care for more details.

Discharge the vortex and filters On a gravity-fed system, all the waste is carried to the filter through the drain at the bottom of the pond. This exposes the filter to a large amount of waste, which if left in the filter would create problems and eventually block the system. It is vital to remove this waste. On a gravity-fed system, cleaning out a particular chamber or vortex, if fitted, is simply a matter of opening the relevant valves and flushing the waste to the main drain.

Weekly

Purge the bottom drain Because a large-bore pipe connects the bottom pond drain to the filter, the water flow through it is quite slow. This means that large, heavy chunks of waste may settle in the pipe and not reach the filter at all. To move this waste it is vital to purge the bottom drain pipe once a week.

Clean the surface skimmers The frequency of cleaning will vary according to the time of year. In the autumn, for example, fallen leaves are likely to cause the biggest blockage in the collecting basket. At any rate, check the skimmer every week and empty the basket if necessary.

Clean the mechanical filter media If you have brushes in the first filter chamber, then clean these every week in the same way as on a pump-fed pond.

Test the water Refer to the section on maintaining water quality (page 96-99) for details on testing.

Monthly

Check and adjust water temperature If you are heating your pond, monitor the temperature every day and adjust it on a month-by-month basis. In temperate regions, it is beneficial to koi to bring the temperature down slightly in the autumn and raise it again in spring. Some floating pond thermometers have a colour zone to indicate the temperature range within which koi are able to accept food.

Adjust aeration Temperature and aeration go hand-in-hand. More aeration is required in the warm summer months and less in the cold winter months.

Half yearly

Change the UV tube As for a pump-fed pond.

Yearly

Clean the filter system Since the filter chambers are regularly discharged to waste, a gravity-fed filter system should not need such a drastic annual overhaul as a pump-fed one. If you check the media chambers and they do not appear to be dirty, leave the relevant discharge valve open for a while so that pond water flows over the media and carries any waste to the drain. Help this process by pouring pond water over the media to dislodge any stubborn waste. Leave the discharge valve open as you do this.

Purging the bottom drain

Follow this sequence to remove heavy waste items that settle in the pipe from the bottom drain to the filter.

1 Turn off the pump
2 Shut off the 110mm (4in) valve to the filter
3 Open the waste valve on the first chamber
4 Wait for the chamber to empty
5 When it is empty, open the 110mm (4in) valve, as shown below
6 Allow the chamber to refill
7 Leave the chamber for 5-10 minutes
8 Open the waste valve on the first chamber to remove the waste

Gravity-fed maintenance

	Daily	Weekly	Monthly	Half yearly	Yearly
Feed the fish	●				
Check fish	●				
Check appliances	●				
Discharge vortex	●				
Discharge filters	●				
Check water temperature	●				
Purge bottom drain		●			
Clean surface skimmers		●			
Clean media		●			
Test water		●			
Adjust water temperature			●		
Adjust aeration			●		
Change UV lamp				●	
Clean out filter system					●

PART THREE

Koi care and maintenance

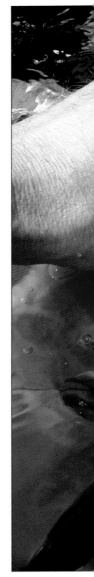

Your pond is built, your koi are swimming around happily in their new home and you can sit back and relax – wrong! Now that your pond is up and running, you will need to devise a routine for yourself so that you can regularly carry out all the tasks required to keep your system in optimum condition. Some jobs, such as feeding the fish, apply to every pond, whereas others depend on the type of filtration you have installed.

You will soon realise that all aspects of koi-keeping are inextricably linked with the efficient running of the pond, however large or small it is and regardless of the complexity of the systems you have installed. For that reason, you should make them part of the everyday regime of dealing with your pond. Set aside a certain time each day to check filters and appliances and to carry out the necessary maintenance quickly. While your fish are feeding, use the opportunity to look them over and keep an eye open for potential health problems. Dedicate

yourself to these tasks and you, your pond and your koi will undoubtedly enjoy the benefits in the long run.

Some people keep koi purely as pets, not too bothered where their fish come from or what they look like. Others start with this attitude, only to realise that the hobby is open-ended. Ponds are then speedily enlarged and upgraded to house quality Japanese fish, and books, magazines and websites are quickly devoured in a steep learning curve to absorb all the latest information. In response to rising demand, a worldwide support industry has grown up to offer quality fish at reasonable prices.

At this stage, the best thing a koi-keeper can do is to join a club, where he or she will benefit from pooled experience. It's a social network, too, as clubs arrange talks, outings and shows, where members' fish are judged against one another. The next stage is the open show circuit, where koi can compete against the best in the land. And breeding your own koi can be the culmination of a dream.

Koi-keeping – the enduring hobby

All modern koi are descendants of carp *(Cyprinus carpio)*, which are indigenous to the Black, Aral, Caspian and Azov Seas of Eastern Asia. The species is highly adaptable and a valuable human food source so, not surprisingly, it spread everywhere that armies marched – across mainland Europe with the Romans and into Britain with the Crusaders around 1550 AD.

The Chinese kept carp five centuries before the birth of Christ, accrediting the fish with near-mystical powers of tenacity. But the story of koi (which simply means 'carp' in Japanese) really began when Chinese forces invaded their island neighbours. Fish were released into the lakes and rivers of Japan, where they thrived – albeit at the expense of some native species, which they out-competed for food.

In the seventeenth century, the peasant rice farmers of Niigata in northern Japan began to culture the introduced Magoi (black carp), which they would dry and salt to sustain their families through the short, but severe, Japanese winters, when small mountain communities were invariably snowed in. The fish were raised in terraced irrigation reservoirs overlooking the paddy fields and harvested in October, before the snows arrived. Larger, parent carp were retained in ponds, some within the farmers' own houses.

The start of koi-keeping

In this sheltered environment, fish with colour abnormalities began to appear. Carp whose black pigment cells (melanophores) were deficient would show a few red or white scales. Instead of these conspicuous fish being picked off by predators, as

would happen in the wild, the farmers crossed them with other mutants to fix these characteristics, purely for curiosity's sake. By the mid-nineteenth century these oddities had achieved pet status. As aquaculture methods improved, and merchants came to Niigata to buy the surplus food fish, the mysterious 'coloured carp' became an open secret among Japan's moneyed classes, who became the first true koi-keepers.

The wider commercial possibilities of koi in their new ornamental role were realised at the 1914 Taisho Exhibition in Tokyo, when 27 coloured carp were publicly displayed. Afterwards, some were gifted to the Emperor for his palace moat, while others were bought by enterprising individuals who guessed there was more money to be made from live fish than dead ones.

Above: *These portly Magoi, or black carp, started it all. Scale mutations arising from inbreeding among fish for the table have resulted in the many colourful, impressive koi varieties we know today.*

It is not certain when koi first arrived in the USA, but the 1941 World Fair in San Francisco featured a large pond of these fish in a Japanese pavilion. Hawaii received its first shipment in 1947. Not until the mid-1960s did koi become available in the UK, largely through the efforts of a fishkeeping businessman who dug holding lakes and teamed up with the owner of a Birmingham-based aquatics outlet to import the fish from the Japanese farmer, Kamihata. With improved air transport and the invention of the plastic bag, which has played a vital role in the successful transportation of koi, this trickle of fish into the UK quickly became a flood.

Above: The indoor koi pool at the Nishikigoi Information Centre, Ojiya. Displays promote the history of koi-keeping, while the gardens feature traditional and modern pond designs.

Left: A mountain scene typical of the area around Niigata, with a terraced mud pond in the distance. Originally, the ponds were used for topping up the rice paddy fields and held carp to supplement the diet.

Koi-keeping – the enduring hobby

Above: *A traditional-style koi pond in Japan. Large moss- and lichen-covered boulders lead down to the water's edge, and the pine and juniper trees in the background are typical elements used to create a Japanese landscape. Note the clarity of the water.*

The modern hobby

In half a century, the quality of Japanese koi has improved immeasurably, with new varieties being developed and existing ones refined. There are metallic koi, plain or multicoloured; partially-scaled Doitsu fish (resulting from crosses with German mirror carp originally bred for the table); Gin-Rin koi with sparkling scales and, most importantly for the true koi devotee, superb modern examples of the 'Big Three' varieties – Kohaku, Sanke and Showa, collectively known as Go Sanke. Careful selection of broodstock, combined with vigorous culling, has brought about better skin quality, more vibrant colours, improved pattern definition and seemingly open-ended growth potential. Sanke have even been back-crossed to Magoi to gain extra show-winning length.

Koi breeders and suppliers

There is still no such thing as a 'typical' koi farmer; some of the best Kohaku continue to be produced part-time by a man with stock ponds in his suburban garage, while at the other end of the scale, Hiroji Sakai's koi farm in Hiroshima is a vast 'production line' facility. However, an infrastructure of breeders, wholesalers and shippers is in place to ensure that the international koi business is on a truly professional footing. Most breeders concentrate on one or two varieties, and all seek to achieve the ultimate accolade – Supreme Champion at the All-Japan Show.

Koi are now farmed worldwide, wherever the climate is suitable. Israel, the USA, China, Cyprus, Indonesia and South Africa are all major producers of koi for the volume market – which demands strong, healthy fish rather than perfect specimens — while Japan remains the homeland of top-quality koi. Major retailers visit the breeders routinely on buying trips, accompanied by hobbyists in search of their dream fish.

Making the most of the hobby

Modern koi-keepers have benefited from the mistakes of those who went before them. When koi first came to the West, it was thought that all they required was an unfiltered garden pond. Now we know that the hobby is really a science, and that koi need sophisticated filtration equipment and large, deep ponds to remain healthy. A vast support industry has duly grown up around koi — specialist dealers, manufacturers of equipment, professional pond builders and magazines devoted solely to these coloured carp.

Koi clubs and societies add the social element, while Internet chatrooms are abuzz with discussions on the best cure for skin blemishes, the merits of wheatgerm pellets or the most economical way to heat a pond through the cold winter period. There has never been a better time to keep koi.

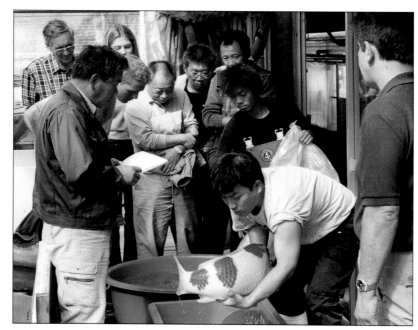

Right: *Koi-handling is an art. Here, a breeder moves a large Kohaku effortlessly from pond to bowl, for closer inspection by potential purchasers. Don't try this with your fish at home!*

Koi anatomy and physiology

In order to understand how best to keep koi, it is necessary to become acquainted with some basic anatomy and physiology. It is only by learning how healthy koi function that we can understand what happens when they become sick, which in turn will help to us to implement an appropriate treatment.

Living in water

Because water is denser than air and more energy is needed to move through it, a koi's body is elegantly streamlined to reduce drag. Furthermore, koi conserve energy in the way they swim. The body musculature literally pulls the tail from side to side and it is the tail that provides the propulsive force that moves the fish forward. Because the water is forced in a stream behind, it creates minute vortices that act together to push the fish forward. The fins act as stabilisers, preventing pitching, rolling and yawing. The pectoral fins also control fine movements at slow speed.

For land animals, breathing air to extract oxygen requires very little effort, but the density of water means that koi use up a large amount of energy to perform the same function. It has been estimated that about 10% of the oxygen they extract from the water is required just to pump water across the gills. The intimate contact between the gills and water presents yet further problems of osmotic and ion regulation (see page 80).

Skin and scales

One of the most characteristic features of any fish is the presence of mucus over the body surface, which makes it feel slimy to the touch. The mucus is not a living tissue but is secreted by the skin and acts as a lubricant as the fish moves through the water, so it is continually sloughed off and replaced. The second function of the mucus is to act as a primary barrier to microbes, including bacteria, viruses, fungus and parasites.

Koi skin consists of two layers. The outermost layer – the epidermis – is a very fine, delicate tissue that lies on the outside of the scales. It forms a barrier between koi and their environment and is responsible for secreting the mucus. The cells of the epidermis multiply on a continuous basis to replace older cells at the surface and repair any injury.

The second layer of skin is called the dermis and contains blood vessels, nerves, connective tissue, certain sense organs and chromatophores – pigmented cells that give rise to the colour patterns. The scales are formed in this layer of skin and if one is lost, a new one is produced by the cells of the dermis. With the exception of doitsu fish, the scales overlap each other rather like roof tiles and provide a flexible, bony protection on the outside of the fish. They are more or less uniform in appearance and shape, apart from those that make up the lateral line.

The lateral line

All fish have a sensory system known as the 'lateral line', a series of scales along each flank with an opening, or pore, visible as a row of dots. The pores open into a canal that runs along the flanks just beneath the scales. Positioned along the inside of each canal are a number of hair cells connected to nerve fibres that relay their impulses to the spinal cord and then to the brain. Any movement of water within the lateral line canals disturbs the hair cells and enables the koi to detect vibrations in the water, which may be reflected off other fish, obstacles or even caused by people's footsteps.

Muscles

Three basic types of muscle are found in all vertebrates: smooth muscle, which is found in the wall of arteries and the larger veins and in the gut, where it is responsible for the movement of food; cardiac, or heart, muscle; and striated, or striped, muscle, which is associated with movement and is attached to the skeleton by gristly tendons. In fish, it is formed into a series of W-shaped blocks called myotomes that encircle the body and provide the thrust for movement.

Body shape and fins

This side view of a young koi shows the basic body shape and the location of the fins and other major external features.

The skeleton

The skeleton is a complex structure with two main functions. The first is to provide support, forming a rigid structure for muscles to attach to, either via tendons directly to bone or via cartilage. Secondly, it provides protection for delicate and sensitive tissues and organs, which are surrounded by bone. For example, the skull encases the brain and eyes.

The digestive system

Instead of teeth in the jaws, koi have paired pharyngeal bones inset with a number of large, molarlike teeth and located just behind the gill arches. The pharyngeal teeth grind food against a cartilaginous pad at the base of the skull. Koi do not have a stomach; the oesophagus simply grades into the intestine (as shown on page 80).

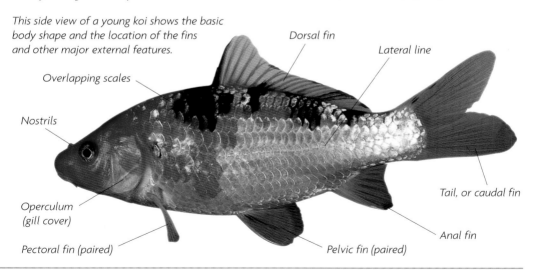

Overlapping scales

Dorsal fin

Lateral line

Nostrils

Operculum (gill cover)

Pectoral fin (paired)

Pelvic fin (paired)

Anal fin

Tail, or caudal fin

Koi anatomy and physiology

Water and salt regulation

In fish, water and salt regulation – also known as osmoregulation – is a very important physiological process. The body fluids and cells of koi contain water and salts in specific amounts and it is important to maintain these concentrations. There is a tendency for water to enter the koi's body continually (primarily through the gill tissue) and for salts inside the body to leach into the surrounding water by diffusion. Koi are able to overcome this problem because their kidneys extract and retain salt from the blood, while removing excess water by producing copious amounts of dilute urine. Water freely enters the body, so koi do not need to drink.

There is also a compromise between the amount of gill tissue that the fish must 'expose' in order to respire efficiently and the 'danger' of exposing too much, thus allowing water to enter the body too freely. Forced exercise, such as that caused by koi-keepers continuously netting the pond, can cause a koi to absorb so much water that its body swells into a state known as dropsy, simply because it is

Internal anatomy

The gills are the site of gas diffusion. Carbon dioxide is released into the water and oxygen is collected by red blood cells. Ammonia is shed by the gill tissue. Essential salts are absorbed by the gills. Water enters the body through the gills.

Sound waves in the water are detected by the swimbladder and amplified by a series of modified backbones, linking them to the inner ear of the koi, enabling it to hear.

The spleen stores immature red blood cells and produces cells of the immune system.

Brain

Koi have very good eyesight.

Barbels (two pairs)

The three-chambered heart (atrium, ventricle and sinus venosus) pumps deoxygenated blood to the gills. The muscular section of the heart, the ventricle, receives oxygen-rich blood from the coronary artery.

The liver is very large. All food digested in the intestine passes to the liver for storage or distribution to the tissues. The liver breaks down unwanted proteins into ammonia, processes old red blood cells and breaks down toxins.

Food is digested in the intestine through the action of enzymes and absorbed by the rich blood supply. Solid waste is voided.

using such a vast area of gill tissue to respire and letting in water during the process.

Gill structure and function

The delicate gills allow oxygen to pass from the water, through the tissue and into the blood, and waste carbon dioxide gas to be released. They are also an important site for excreting nitrogenous waste, with 82% being eliminated as ammonia and 8% as urea. The remaining 10% is excreted by the kidneys as urea in the form of dilute urine.

The swimbladder

The primary function of the swimbladder is to control buoyancy. In koi, the swimbladder primitively retains a connection to the gut and, indeed, the fish can top up the gas content of this organ by gulping air at the water surface. More usually, the gas content of the swimbladder is controlled by a number of blood vessels.

In koi (as in many other fish), the swimbladder also fulfils a role in amplifying sound and relaying it to the inner ear via a series of small bones.

Backbone

The paired kidneys conserve salts in the body and produce vast amounts of very dilute urine to remove water and maintain an osmotic balance in the body.

The swimbladder is a gas-filled buoyancy organ that allows the koi to remain at any depth in the water using the minimum amount of energy. The gas inside is mostly oxygen, as this is taken from the blood supply. When the koi wants to reach the pond surface to feed, gas is added to the swimbladder. When swimming to the bottom, gas is removed.

The gonads, or reproductive organs, are situated on either side of the body. The ovaries produce eggs and can be very large. The testes produce sperm (milt).

The vent describes the area of the body where the intestine opens at the anus and where urine from the kidneys is released and eggs or sperm (milt) are shed into the water through the urogenital opening.

Buying and introducing koi

Buying koi is both a pleasure and a commitment, as all ornamental fish deserve the same high level of care. Accepting losses of cheap koi before filter systems are fully matured is indefensible. Only when you are certain that you can provide a stress-free environment should you start to build your own koi collection.

Buying koi is not as time-sensitive as it once was, thanks to improvements in shipping techniques and overseas holding facilities. And, if you heat your pond, newly imported koi will not struggle to adapt to a change in climate. Today, it is possible to fly to Japan to select fish at source from their breeders, or even to buy koi over the Internet. However, a visit in person to a reputable dealer is still the first choice for most koi-keepers.

Below: *The Internet can give some idea of fish available for sale, but however good the images, this is no substitute for seeing the koi first-hand.*

Country of origin

It makes sense to buy the best koi you can. Long-term, the cost of fish will be small compared to the outlay on their pond and associated equipment, plus the ongoing bills for their upkeep.

Japanese koi are the finest in the world, and in real terms represent the best value for money. Fish from Israel, the USA, South Africa, China, Singapore and Cyprus all have their devotees. But only in Japan are experienced breeders able to capitalise on the long, hot summers and the unique mineral content of their mud ponds, essential to good growth and skin quality. Even ordinary-grade Japanese fish compare favourably with the best koi from other countries and are a good choice for those who merely want a colourful display. As quality improves, the asking price rises, but balancing what you want against what you can afford is all part of the fascination of the hobby.

When to buy

The Japanese net their mud ponds in late October/early November, and that is when the finest fish become available. Coincidentally, autumn temperatures best suit koi in transit, but even at other times of the year, sophisticated packing techniques and gradual temperature adjustment still ensure a safe journey in the aircraft's cargo hold.

It is common practice for dealers to travel out to hand-pick quality koi from the autumn harvest on behalf of their customers, or acquire a whole pondful of fish at favourable rates. Hobbyists in search of something really special can accompany these koi professionals to Japan. The fish they choose are either shipped back home or, for a fee,

Left: Your koi will be with you for a long time, so choose them carefully. View them in strong, natural daylight, at close quarters and don't be rushed or influenced by sales talk. The important thing is that you like what you are buying.

Where to buy

Reputable koi dealers may not always tell you what you would like to hear, or even refuse to sell you any fish until they are convinced your pond is suitable. Don't be put off by this. It means they care about their livestock and in the longer term they will be a valuable source of advice and assistance in return for your regular custom.

If possible, buy koi only from specialist dealers. Long-established koi businesses pose the fewest risks, but new ones are being set up all the time. If you visit a new dealership, be guided by first impressions. Are the premises well laid-out and tidy? Do the staff use separate nets for each pond or vat and disinfect them between use? Does the dealer stock all the necessary ancillary equipment as well as fish? The holding water should be well-filtered and clear, as much for the well-being of the koi as for ease of viewing. If in doubt, go elsewhere.

Buying koi through the web

Many koi retailers worldwide now have their own website, or webpage. Koi are described in detail, along with a picture, so that prospective buyers can

remain with the breeders for a further year or more to grow on. The risk is borne by the buyer, but the rewards can be great. Some dealers revisit Japan in the spring to buy the remainder of the koi from the autumn harvest. These represent real bargains. If Japanese holding facilities are available, fish can be released in batches to satisfy demand throughout the summer.

Ordinary and middle-grade koi tend to be handled more by wholesalers and buying co-operatives. They will offer guaranteed prices to breeders who can consistently supply colourful, healthy stock. These koi are available all year round, especially in the smaller sizes.

Owners of heated ponds and quarantine tanks can safely buy koi at any time. For the rest, it is better to pay for selected fish and board them with the dealer until outside water temperatures stabilise above 10°C (50°F).

Buying and introducing koi

make an astute choice, even though they have not seen a fish 'in the flesh'. If the retailer has a known and trusted outlet, buyers may even acquire the koi over the web. The fish is then despatched via a courier service for immediate delivery. However, even the best photographic images can give a misleading impression, so be cautious about buying koi without seeing them first.

Trusted koi retailers can select a fish on your behalf while visiting Japan. During their seasonal buying trips, many dealers take digital photographs of any exceptional koi and these photographs are then downloaded onto a computer and emailed across the world to the retail outlet, or even directly to the customer to consider.

Transporting koi

Having made your selection, ask the dealer to bag the fish for you. Before the bag is sealed, lift it up to the light and make one final check on the koi, paying special attention to the belly region. Examine the eyes and barbels, and satisfy yourself that there are no deformities of the mouth and jawbone, a common fault in Showa, for example.

The double or triple bag should contain just enough clean transit water to cover the koi's back, with the remaining space inflated from an oxygen cylinder. For long journeys, the dealer will sometimes add a soothing, mildly antiseptic agent. The bag is then sealed with rubber bands.

Once you have paid for your koi, it is your responsibility to get it home safely. Fish travel best in the dark, so wrap the bag in a black plastic bin liner and lay it on its side in a stout cardboard box or, better still, a large polystyrene container with a

Bagging up your chosen koi

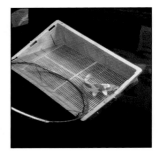

1 This Kujaku has been singled out as a possible purchase. It is gently tipped from a catching net into a floating viewing basket and brought nearer to the prospective buyer for a closer inspection.

2 From above it looks good – blemish-free, good skin and pattern, and it deports well in the confines of the basket. Ask questions if you are unsure.

The koi is upended by the dealer so that its underside can be checked, too.

3 When you are satisfied, the dealer will bag the koi, but before the bag is sealed check the koi once again to make sure that all is well.

4 The koi is double-bagged with just enough water to cover its back, while the remainder of the space is taken up by oxygen from a cylinder. It will now go into a polybox for, ideally, a swift journey to its home pond.

Buying koi checklist

Plus points
- Good body shape and skin quality
- Well-distributed pattern the full length of the body (in varieties such as Showa)
- Clear, well-shaped head
- Fins in proportion to body
- Bilateral symmetry
- Straight spine
- Good, lively deportment

Minus points
- Badly split fins; missing fins (usually a pelvic fin)
- Reddened vent or raised, angry scales (both signs of bacterial infection)
- Scars or missing scales below the lateral line (not visible when koi is viewed from above)
- Anchor worm (Argulus) parasites
- Fungus
- Broken dorsal and/or pectoral fin rays
- Clamped fins
- Gills not working at the same rate or too-rapid, indicating gill damage
- Damaged/missing eye(s)
- Eroded or reddened barbels
- Listless behaviour
- Erratic swimming
- Head-up/head-down position in the water
- Excessively thin body, especially just behind gills
- Rough feel to body (indicating lack of protective mucus)
- Part-missing or outcurled gill covers

General
- Ask whether the fish is male or female (you do not want to pay for a female, only to find that it is a male).
- Closely examine any fish, first in a bowl, then by holding up the bag to examine the underside and to check that all fins are present and correct.

Buying and introducing koi

lid. The insulating properties of the polybox should maintain an even water temperature during the journey, but on very warm days, one or more coolpacks from the freezer, wrapped in newspaper or a blanket, will provide added protection.

If the koi are large, lay the wrapped bags or boxes lengthways across the car boot or in the footwell behind the front seats where they cannot shift around. Do not carry the boxes in the front footwell or on a passenger's lap, where they will get too warm and be vulnerable in the event of an accident. Avoid unnecessary stops on the journey and drive smoothly, cornering gently and taking the most direct route home.

On arrival, open the bag, or bags, roll down the tops to form a collar and float them on the surface of the pond or quarantine facility. This is purely to equalise water temperatures and should take no

more than 20 minutes. Open the bag and carefully lift the fish out by hand or use a koi sock if it is too large to handle. Introduce the fish into the pond and discard the water in the bag.

If the fish go into a relatively low-volume quarantine vat (see panel opposite), it is important to take an ammonia reading an hour or two later. Koi have a tendency to 'dump' ammonia when they are moved from dirty into clean water, and you should perform a large partial water change through a purifier to dilute this toxin. Leave the new arrivals undisturbed, and on no account feed them for a couple of days. If possible, net over the pond or vat,

Below: *When you spot a likely purchase, observe its behaviour. It should swim with a fluid motion in the company of other koi. Until you gain experience, ask a seasoned koi-keeper to accompany you.*

A quarantine facility

The quarantine facility should provide an impeccable pond environment on a small scale. You can buy a ready-made system, but most hobbyists prefer to build their own in a garage or outhouse. Aim for a minimum of 2,250 litres (500 gallons). A popular choice is a floor-level blockwork shell, either rendered and fibreglassed or with a crease-free box-welded liner dropped in. Although they are inadequate for koi ponds, 'black box' filters come into their own for quarantining fish, as they can cope well with small volumes of water and are easy to service. As with all filters, make sure that they are fully matured before introducing any koi.

When you first fill the quarantine vat, run the water through a purifier and record the capacity with a flowmeter (see page 52). This ensures that in future you can administer accurate doses of any necessary medication.

The vat should be heated. If your pond is heated by gas, you can run a loop from the system; otherwise, use an inline electric heater. The temperature should be kept at 16°C (61°F) or above, for several reasons. Firstly, warmth speeds up the life cycle of parasites, so that any latent infestation will show itself quickly. At the same time, the immune system of the koi will be fully geared up. Tissue healing, biological filter efficiency and the viability of some medications are all dependent on higher temperatures, and finally, the appetite of healthy fish kept warm will be good.

The quarantine vat should also be well aerated and free from any projections on which koi might injure themselves. To save on electricity, insulate the walls with thick sheets of polystyrene and install a ventilated cover that will conserve heat and prevent the fish jumping out.

as koi have a tendency to jump until they have become acclimatised to their new surroundings.

The quarantine issue

Dealer quarantine (withholding fish from sale for some weeks) allows koi time to recuperate from the stress of their journey. Run-down koi are susceptible to ailments they would normally shrug off, but in a warm vat the commoner protozoan parasites (especially white spot) will soon manifest themselves and can be successfully treated. However, other, more serious diseases have a longer incubation period, or can be triggered by environmental factors. Dealer quarantine alone is no guarantee that a fish is not carrying an infection that could easily wipe out a whole pond. A few dealers choose not to quarantine new arrivals. This is acceptable, provided they make it quite clear to their customers, and as long as obviously stressed fish are not offered for sale.

The main argument against quarantining at home is that it necessitates yet one more stressful change of environment for the koi, rather than a direct transfer from the dealer's vats to your pond.

Feeding your koi

Feeding your koi will become one of the most enjoyable aspects of your hobby, and gives you a chance to appreciate the fish at least once a day (but see later for more advice on feeding regimes). The amount and type of food you give your koi will largely depend on the water temperature. If the pond is heated to a minimum of 14°C (57°F) all year round, you have the advantage of being able to feed the fish throughout the year. Not only will this enable you to watch them all year round, but it also helps you to achieve amazing growth rates. If the pond is not heated, monitor the water temperature and stop feeding altogether when it drops below 8°C (46°F). In water temperatures of 8-14°C (46-57°F), offer the koi a lower-protein food, such as wheatgerm, which they can digest more easily. At temperatures above 14°C (57°F), feed them on a standard staple food, and in the very warmest months, add specialist colour or growth-enhancing foods.

Koi food is available in all shapes and sizes, from sticks and pellets to paste and even sinking varieties.

The type of food you give your koi is a matter of personal choice, but bear in mind that as in most things, you get what you pay for in terms of quality.

The most popular types of food include floating pellets and sticks, which are widely available. Many different ingredients are included in these foods, all designed to improve the health, condition and colour of your fish. Several food additives are available that provide further nutritional benefits.

When feeding your koi it is best to offer them small amounts several times a day, rather than one or two large feeds. As a guide, provide enough food so that none is left after three to five minutes. In the colder months a single feed each day will be sufficient, but in the hotter summer months you can feed the fish four or five times a day, as well as offering treats such as prawns and oranges. Adding some sinking food to the staple diet encourages the koi to feed at different levels in the pond, thus reducing the risk of your prize koi damaging each other when they all rush to the surface.

Left: *Lettuce is a valuable source of Vitamin C and other nutrients. Start by offering shredded leaves; in a short time, the koi will enjoy chasing a whole lettuce around the pond and tearing off pieces. Oranges are another treat, but remove uneaten items before they decompose.*

Below: *Koi are totally dependent on their owners for food. They need a good-quality, varied diet that takes into account water temperature, and the size, weight and number of fish in the pond. Overfeeding puts a heavy load on the filtration system.*

Feeding your koi

Dried foods

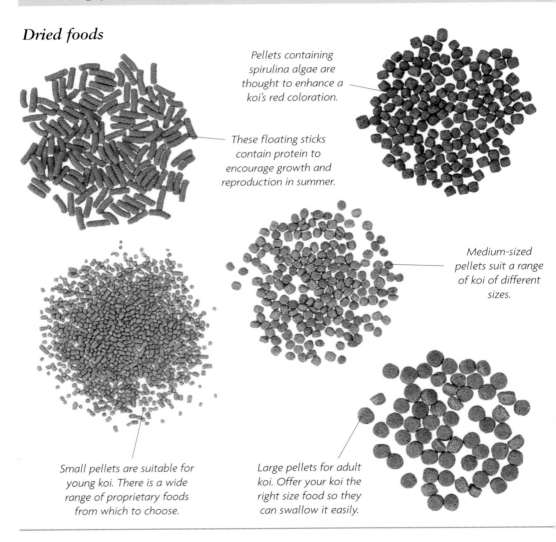

Pellets containing spirulina algae are thought to enhance a koi's red coloration.

These floating sticks contain protein to encourage growth and reproduction in summer.

Medium-sized pellets suit a range of koi of different sizes.

Small pellets are suitable for young koi. There is a wide range of proprietary foods from which to choose.

Large pellets for adult koi. Offer your koi the right size food so they can swallow it easily.

Left: Pelleted, flake and other dried foods provide koi with a well-balanced diet. However, be aware that formulations vary, so check the ingredients carefully. Store foods in airtight containers and do not carry them over from one season to the next.

Oranges provide Vitamin C. The koi will cluster eagerly round the segments, eating everything but the peel.

Below: Wholemeal or granary bread is a good source of wheatgerm and vitamins, but it is rich in carbohydrate so feed it sparingly. Peas and sweetcorn are also high-carbohydrate foods that make the fish excessively fat.

Feeding your koi

Preparing paste food

1 This food is supplied as a fine powder. Follow the instructions and measure out the amount needed to make one day's food ration.

2 Using the supplied measuring cup for convenience, slowly add enough tapwater to the powder to make it moist but not too wet.

3 Mix the powder and water together until it has a dough-like consistency. Add more water as needed to create a soft paste.

4 Knead the paste in your hands and peel off lumps of food to feed your koi. Make the pieces a suitable size for your koi and simply throw them in the pond.

Below: Young koi chasing an orange segment around the surface of their pond. They will eat the flesh of the fruit with enthusiasm until only the clean peel remains. Remove this to prevent it rotting in the water.

Mixing an additive with koi food

1 Measure out enough feed for one or two days. This is a staple pelleted food suitable for everyday feeding.

2 Add water to the food to make it just moist. This will help it to absorb the additive more effectively.

3 Stir the food to ensure that it all comes into contact with the water. Use a large bowl to prevent spillage.

4 Following the directions, measure out the appropriate amount of the additive. This one confers health, colour-enhancing and growth benefits.

5 Mix the food thoroughly to ensure an even covering of the additive. Then leave it for a few minutes to allow the additive to soak in and the pellets to dry out.

6 Feed the treated food to your koi but ensure that it is used within one or two days. This is to ensure that it is fresh and the full benefits are gained.

Health care

Make a habit of checking your koi every day at feeding time. This will enable you to see that they are all present and behaving normally. When they come up to the surface you can inspect them closely for any signs of damage or disease.
If there seems to be a general disease problem, you can dose the whole pond with a suitable treatment. The presence of parasites, for example, may be indicated by the fish flicking against the bottom or sides of the pond.

General anti-parasite treatments are available; always follow the manufacturer's guidance on dosing rates. You must measure out these medications accurately, taking into account the exact volume of your pond; make sure you know what it is (see page 201). If you underdose, the medication simply will not work and overdosing may have a harmful effect on the koi. Buy a good measuring cylinder or set of

Above: *Measure any medication carefully and never add it to the pond in concentrated form. Fill a plastic watering can with pond water, add the correct amount of medication and stir. Gently sprinkle on the pond surface.*

gram balances to measure out the appropriate medication, be it liquid or powder. If possible, take a mucus scrape from an affected fish and examine it under a microscope to determine the exact parasite. This allows you to select the best medication.

If just one or two koi have raised or lost scales or small wounds, this may indicate that there is an area

---

Koi herpes virus

In recent years, outbreaks of koi herpes virus (KHV) have caused mortalities amongst koi in many parts of the world. The virus is spread through contact with infected koi and their body fluids, plus water or filter waste from infected systems. Other pond fish, such as orfe and goldfish, are not affected by the virus and do not seem to be carriers.

Many diseases produce symptoms similar to those of KHV but usually there is sloughing of the skin, accompanied by erosion of the gills and mortalities. The only way to identify the disease is by submitting koi tissues from suspected infections for virology and histopathology. Koi infected with KHV can mount an immune response and recover, but remain infected for life; if they are stressed they can suffer recurring bouts of infection and spread the disease months or even years after the initial infection. As there is no cure for a viral infection it is best to isolate all new koi for about 14 days at 20-27°C (68-80°F), which is the incubation period for KHV, before introducing them to the main pond.

Treating a koi with propolis

1 A typical small wound or ulcer on koi.

2 Anaesthetise the koi and carefully clean the affected site with a cotton wool bud.

3 Treat the cleaned area with propolis spray until it is fully covered. This will be absorbed into the surface tissues, not only disinfecting the area but also stopping bacteria penetrating the tissues any further.

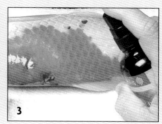

Above: Allow the propolis to dry and form a protective coating over the affected area. Then place the koi back into the pond in a floating basket near an airstone. Repeat this every two to three days, or as needed. If the problems persist, seek expert help.

or object in the pond on which the fish are damaging themselves. Carefully take out the affected fish and treat any wounds individually. If the fish is large or awkward to handle, you may need to anaesthetise it to reduce the levels of stress involved. Find out how the damage occurred and take steps to prevent it happening again. Raised or lost scales may reflect damage caused by flicking due to parasites or an increased level of bacteria in the pond, in which case more general treatment of the water is necessary. If you experience this, seek professional advice, as a bacterial swab may need to be taken and cultured in a laboratory to determine the exact nature of the problem.

Maintaining water quality

At the very least, test your pond water for ammonia, nitrite and pH every week. Most problems arise in some way from poor water quality and regular testing enables you to pinpoint irregularities quickly so that you can take any necessary remedial action. Try to get into the habit of regular water testing and, ideally, also include tests for dissolved oxygen level (particularly in warm weather), nitrate and general water hardness.

Ammonia test

Below: *To test pond water for the presence of ammonia, compare a sample against the colours on the chart supplied.*

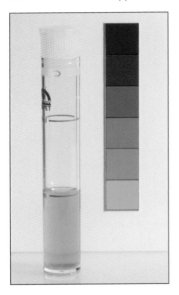

How the nitrogen cycle works

Water returning to the pond from the last stage of the filtration system may still contain some nitrate. Nitrate is one of the nutrients responsible for promoting the growth of blanketweed.

By adding an oxygen atom into each molecule, aerobic bacteria (Nitrobacter spp.) convert nitrite into nitrate (NO$_3$). Nitrate is the final breakdown product of ammonia in the nitrogen cycle and far less toxic than ammonia or nitrite.

By removing the hydrogen and adding oxygen into each molecule, aerobic bacteria (Nitrosomonas spp.) convert ammonia into nitrite (NO$_2$). Although not as harmful as ammonia, it is still very poisonous to koi.

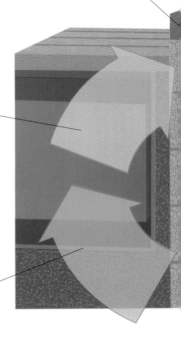

Water changes are an important aspect of pond management, especially if ammonia or nitrite are polluting the pond. Regular water changes can also help to reduce nitrate concentration in the water.

Protein supplied in food is used by koi for tissue repair and maintenance, growth and reproduction. Any excess protein cannot be stored and is excreted as ammonia. The protein in any uneaten food also ends up as ammonia.

Nitrite test

Below: Nitrite, the secondary breakdown product of ammonia, is also extremely poisonous to koi. High levels often occur in new ponds before the nitrogen cycle is fully established. Monitor the pond and carry out partial water changes.

Ammonia (NH$_3$) is released into the water by the gills. The small amount of urea voided in dilute urine breaks down to form ammonia. Ammonia is very poisonous to koi.

Maintaining water quality

Broad range pH test

Above: It is vital to test the pH of the water routinely, as this will affect the toxicity of ammonia. The ideal pH range for the koi pond is between 6.5 and 8.5, so a broad range test kit is ideal. Here, a small tablet is mixed with 10ml of pond water and the colour compared to a chart.

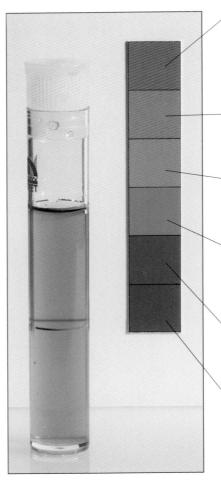

pH 4 Too acidic – koi unwell, not feeding. In hard water, increase pH by water changes. In soft water, make partial water changes, add marble chippings, oyster shell or chalk-based minerals/clays.

pH 5 pH still too low – koi will be lethargic. Increase pH as described above.

pH 6.5 Preferred pH range is 6.5-8.5, but even at this level, it could be increased.

pH 7 Pure or distilled water is pH 7, but unlikely to be achieved in the koi pond. Distilled water is devoid of minerals/salts.

pH 8.5 Top value recommended for koi. Does not cause them any major problems.

pH 9 In planted ponds, or those affected by algae blooms, the pH can rise above 9 to about 11 during the day, but causes few welfare or health problems.

Phosphate test

1 Add 5 drops of the phosphate reagent to a 5ml sample of pond water and shake gently to mix.

2 Allow the sample to stand until the yellow colour has fully developed and then compare it with the chart. Place the tube on the printed chart and look down the length of the tube to compare the colour of the solution.

3 A reading of 0mg/litre (far right) is ideal. Control medium to high levels with partial water changes.

Dissolved oxygen test

Oxygen is essential for koi and a number of factors, including water temperature and the number of fish in the pond, can adversely affect dissolved oxygen levels.

2 Swirl the solution until it is an even colour.

3 Add the final reagent one drop at a time.

1 Stabilise the oxygen content by adding a series of reagents. At this point, a further reagent causes the test sample to turn black.

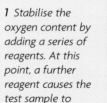

4 Count the drops until the solution is clear for the oxygen reading.

Breeding koi

When koi hobbyists talk of breeding their koi, it is a very different affair from what goes on in Japan, or anywhere these fish are produced commercially.

Flock spawnings

Flock, or uncontrolled, spawnings in koi ponds will occur spontaneously, provided sexually mature males and females are present, water temperature and light levels have been high enough and long enough ('degree days'), and there is a medium within which eggs can be laid and fertilised. However, many spawnings go unnoticed, because the parent koi immediately devour the eggs. Except in heavily planted ponds (or those with an unacceptably dense cover of blanketweed), any stray, free-swimming fry will soon be picked off. Brood survival depends on the koi-keeper intervening before the eggs hatch, separating them and then providing spacious accommodation and limitless live food as soon as the fry are able to take it.

The quality of flock-spawned 'home-breds' is generally very disappointing; the young fish display poor body shape and ill-defined patterns. The

success rate is improved somewhat in the case of the less complex varieties: metallics crossed with metallics, or Chagoi with Chagoi. A few individuals will then develop into quite passable pond fish, though seldom reach show standard. Spawnings of Kohaku, Sanke and Showa are much more hit-and-miss, because there is no way of knowing their gene pool: handsome parents do not automatically produce good-looking progeny.

This is not to say that breeding your own koi is not fascinating. It can be a worthwhile exercise, if only because ripe females are rid of spawn that they would otherwise have to re-absorb.

Planned spawnings

Planned spawnings involve pairings between selected parents, which are kept apart and conditioned. When they are put together again, it is in a controlled and observed environment, so that eggs deposited on a spawning rope or brush can be removed before they are eaten. The rope is then placed in a rearing facility as before.

In Japan, parent koi are beyond price, and the breeders will have years of experimentation behind them, which gives them a good idea of which fish to put together to obtain the best results. Even so, massive fry cullings take place before even ordinary-grade fish emerge, and from an initial spawning, perhaps only a dozen koi will be true Tategoi (fine

Left: *Flock spawning is a boisterous business. There is no control over which sperm joins with which egg, and surviving fry are unlikely to bear much resemblance to their parents, though there is always an outside chance.*

fish with scope for further improvement).

To rear koi through this scrupulous selection process requires pond space and funds unavailable to ordinary hobbyists. So, next time you complain about the price of a fish, it is worth remembering the work that went into producing it.

Basic genetics

A koi will receive one gene from each parent for each characteristic. It cannot receive two genes from one and none from the other. If you mate a scaled koi with a scaleless (Doitsu) koi, you might expect to produce some of each type, but this is not always the case. One gene can mask the other completely – known as a dominant gene masking a recessive one. When breeding a particular variety of koi, you must first select suitable broodstock (parent fish). Like the breeders in Japan, select one suitable female to at least three males to ensure a successful spawning. The chosen parents, both male and female, need not be perfect in every respect (variety, colour, shape, deportment, etc.). If you require good colour, then select a koi for that feature alone; the fish's other attributes can be secondary. Over several seasons, you will be able to introduce all the prime features into the offspring.

A spawning rope

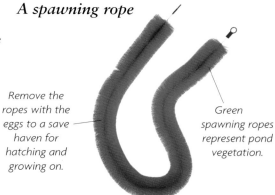

Remove the ropes with the eggs to a save haven for hatching and growing on.

Green spawning ropes represent pond vegetation.

A floating spawning cage

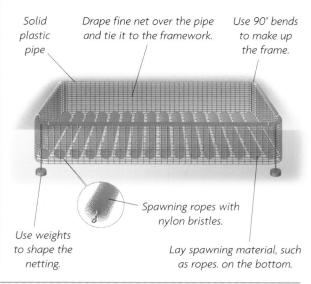

Solid plastic pipe

Drape fine net over the pipe and tie it to the framework.

Use 90° bends to make up the frame.

Spawning ropes with nylon bristles.

Use weights to shape the netting.

Lay spawning material, such as ropes. on the bottom.

Showing koi

An obsession with showing koi is a quality shared by all top Japanese breeders and many hobbyists worldwide. To win the All-Japan Show is the dream of all serious koi producers, for emotional as well as financial reasons, while success at a hobby show confirms that fish are being kept properly and are reaching their full potential. Showing is also an opportunity to make a realistic comparison of your koi-keeping skills with those of others, and to meet like-minded people.

Aside from club shows, where entry is limited to members' koi, open shows tend to be held under the auspices of a governing body. In the USA it is the Associated Koi Clubs of America, in Japan and countries where there are affiliated chapters it is the ZNA (Zen Nippon Airinkai), while in the UK the British Koi Keepers Society (BKKS) holds sway. All these associations have 'apprentice' judges, trained to a uniformly high standard over many years before achieving full status.

What happens at a koi show

An open koi show follows one of two main formats. In one case, all koi of the same size and variety are exhibited in the same vat and moved around as the show progresses. In the second, each entrant has his or her own vats (holding facilities) in which the koi remain throughout the judging process. This option reduces the likelihood of disease transmission, but is more cumbersome to administer and harder for the judging team.

There are currently 13 judging classes and seven size categories in BKKS shows. A 'class', as this book reveals, may be single variety (e.g. Kohaku) or multiple variety (e.g. Hikarimoyo, which includes

Above: Part of the benching process involves measuring koi before they are entered into their size class (one of seven categories). This Showa will be held against the measuring scale to ensure fair play.

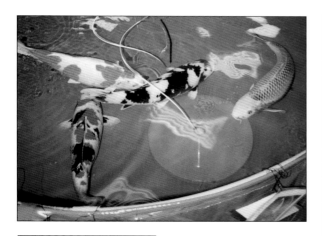

Above: Same size, but different varieties – the Japanese show format is easiest on the judges.

Above: At a provincial English koi show, a senior judge works alongside a trainee so that the less experienced member of the team can be instructed and continuously assessed. Becoming a full judge can take three years or more.

Above: Booking in koi at the All-Japan Show near Tokyo is carried out with production line efficiency. Dealers help out with this task.

Left: Koi are taken to their show vats in wheeled trolleys such as this, and rarely is a drop of water spilled on the way.

Showing koi

several types of metallic fish of more than one colour). The aim is always the same — to judge like against like fairly, culminating in the major awards of best baby, adult and mature koi. The overall supreme champion is chosen from these; in 99 percent of cases, this will be a large fish and either a Kohaku, a Sanke or a Showa.

Preparing for a show

To stand a good chance in open competition, you should first show your koi at club level. This will give some indication of their merit (and opinions may be at odds with those of their blinkered owner!). If the fish cross that hurdle, then to progress further in the show world, they need the right treatment if they are to look their best. As well as providing good basic pond husbandry and plenty of swimming space, feed them colour-enhancing foods as part of a varied diet. Heated ponds are vital to ensure that the koi attain a good size while they still have youthful skin, and of course, no koi should be entered into a show if it is in any way diseased, deformed, injured or carrying visible parasites.

A responsible koi-owner will ensure that the fish arrive at a show in good condition, but once they are benched (sorted according to size and variety), responsibility for their welfare passes to the organisers. At the end of the show, when the koi are de-benched and returned to their owners, it is essential that all the facilities are there for a safe and stress-free journey home. It is up to the hobbyist to provide oxygen, plastic bags and transport boxes to ensure that this happens.

Many koi-keepers are not show minded, while others feel that the stress of moving fish around the country, however minimal, cannot be justified by the winning of rosettes and trophies. However, there is little doubt that the showing fraternity tends to own the best fish, and advances the hobby by pushing for ever-higher standards of koi and the means to keep them in the best conditions.

When using montmorillionite clay to replenish essential minerals in the pond, disperse it into a bucket of pond water before introducing it into the surface skimmer. You can also add this directly to the food to give your koi an extra sparkle before a show.

Above: Regular meals of colour-enhancing pellets delivered through an auto-feeder are a good pre-show tactic. Follow this by a period of fasting.

Right: Grand Champion of the 2001 All-Japan show, a 90cm (36in) Kohaku owned by a Taiwanese hobbyist. Such youthful skin and deep, clearly-defined hi (red) are exceptional in such a large koi.

PART FOUR

Koi colour varieties

Beginners will frequently ask of a particular koi: "What species is that?" The question merits only one valid reply – *Cyprinus carpio* – because that is the scientific name carried by all koi, however diverse they appear to be in their colour and pattern.

So, is the word 'breed' more appropriate? It works for pedigree dogs, in the sense that if you cross a corgi with another corgi, more corgis result. But, with koi, the outcome is nowhere near as certain. Put a male and a female Sanke together and the resulting fry will certainly contain a percentage of Sanke – plus Bekko, Kohaku and many nondescripts.

The terms used to describe koi are 'class' and 'variety'. These are purely arbitrary, as the fish have all been developed by man, but they do at least give us a yardstick by which koi can be bought and judged. Each class may contain one or many varieties. For example, Kohaku, Sanke and Showa are single-variety classes, whereas the Kawarimono class is home to dozens of non-metallic koi

that do not readily slot elsewhere into the hierarchy. To confuse the issue further, there are subvarieties, with a Japanese terminology that distinguishes them from other, broadly similar, fish. To take the example of Kohaku, there are terms for two, three and four-step pattern koi; words to describe their scalation; and others that relate to markings. So a Doitsu Sandan Maruten Kuchibeni Kohaku would be a white and red non-metallic koi (Kohaku) with mirror scales (Doitsu), three-step pattern (Sandan), including a separate patch of red on the head (Maruten), and red lips (Kuchibeni).

Recognising all the varieties takes time, and there will always be some koi that spark disputes, even among so-called 'experts'. More important is to recognise a healthy, well-shaped koi with good skin.

The enduring appeal of koi is that no two are alike. The impact of the colours and patterns, on single fish or in the company of others, determines the mood of the collection.

KOHAKU

Kohaku are white koi with red (hi) patterning. This deceptively simple, yet inspiring, combination makes them the most sought-after variety in the world. Many beginners are initially attracted by this minimalism, only to be lured away by more extravagantly arrayed, metallic fish. But the true connoisseur will come back to Kohaku with a heightened appreciation of the limitless interplay between two primary colours. No two Kohaku are alike, and that explains the fascination.

Patterns may be delicate and flowery (komoyo), or bold and imposing (omoyo). In either instance, quality Kohaku, particularly when large, convey the impression of quiet, graceful elegance, and rightly dominate the major awards in shows.

The Japanese have been breeding this variety for more than 100 years, over which time it has improved almost beyond recognition. It is one of only two types of koi (the other is Sanke) with traceable bloodlines, though pedigree is only one consideration among many when choosing Kohaku. At best it is a pointer, never a cast-iron guarantee, as to how a fish may develop. It is short-sighted to purchase only from breeders currently in the public eye – to do so is to miss out on some potential gems from lesser-known koi farms.

Three marks of a good Kohaku

The desirable elements in a top-class Kohaku are good body shape, skin quality and pattern. Of these, only skin quality is immediately apparent in young fish – beginners tend to confuse this with colour, which is quite another concept. 'Finished' hi (the stable colour of an adult fish) should be a

Left: *One of the best koi in the world!*
This 90cm (36in) Maruten Kohaku was
Grand Champion at the 2001 All-Japan
Show. All elements are near perfect,
especially the voluminous body shape.

Below: *In a young Kohaku such as this one,*
body potential is hard to assess. However,
skin quality, pattern and depth of hi already
mark out this koi as one to keep an eye on.

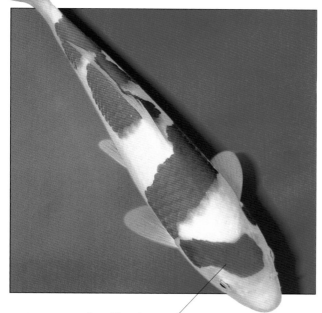

Opposing angles of head hi and
the first pattern step highlight the
pure white shoulders.

The history of Kohaku

Red-and-white mutations of the
ancestral black carp (Magoi) first
appeared in the early 1800s among
fish bred for food by rice farmers in
Niigata prefecture. For curiosity's
sake, rather than with any thoughts
of commercial gain, the farmers
kept these back as pets and
spawned them together. 'Kohaku-
like' characteristics emerged in
some of these offspring – red
heads, gill covers and lips, or small
patches of hi on the back and belly,
though nothing worthy of being
called a pattern. That changed in
1888, when Kunizo Hiroi ran a red-
headed female koi with one of his
own male fish, whose markings
resembled cherry blossoms. The
resulting fry were used by other
breeders to establish the now
extinct Gosuke bloodline. All
subsequent Kohaku bloodlines
(Tomoin, Sensuke, Yagozen, Manzo)
arose from fish of Gosuke lineage
outcrossed to unrelated fish
showing promise. They were
named after the breeders who
refined their koi over many
generations of careful selection.
Tomoin and Yagozen are the two
major bloodlines today.

KOHAKU

deep orange-red, but young Kohaku – even of the highest grade – that have not yet been given colour-enhancing food may look very insipid.

High-quality skin is difficult to describe, but unmistakable once seen. 'Lustre', 'depth', 'clarity' and 'purity' are all relevant attributes – good white skin carries a blemish-free sheen, as though the fish had been given several coats of silk emulsion paint.

Body shape changes as the koi grows. Young fish of both sexes are slim, but pointers to a Kohaku that will attain good volume in later life are a thick caudal peduncle (wrist of the tail) and broad shoulders. As to size, you cannot expect the koi to grow large unless it comes from large parent stock – this is where known bloodline comes into play.

Pattern, the third element, is what gives every Kohaku its unique character. The Japanese once laid down strict formal guidelines as to where the hi should be positioned on the white skin, and fish that fell outside these parameters were not highly valued. Today's attitude is far more relaxed, although the 'step' classification is still used for convenience – Nidan (two-step), Sandan (three-step), Yondan (four-step) and Godan (five-step). A 'step' is a stand-alone patch of hi anywhere on the head or body of the fish, but single, random red scales do not qualify.

All-important hi

Kohaku hi originates on the back of the fish and extends down over the flanks, as opposed to the 'wrapping' type of pattern seen in Showa, which can encircle the abdomen. When choosing Kohaku, it is important to understand that blocks of hi may 'break'. A young fish whose pattern resembles that of an accomplished adult may not have enough hi to see it

Step-patterned Kohaku

Nidan (two-step) Kohaku are typically unfussy, yet imposing, koi of the traditional type.

Sandan (three-step) Kohaku should strike a good balance between the plain and the flowery pattern types.

Well-shaped, pure white pectoral fins enhance any Kohaku.

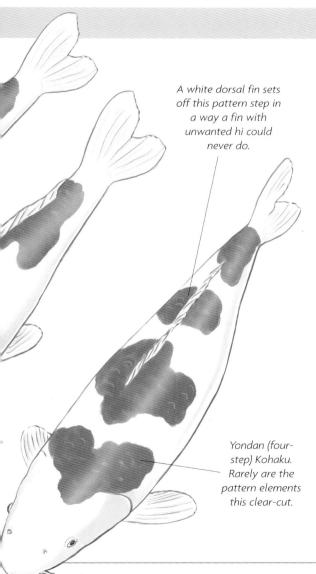

A white dorsal fin sets off this pattern step in a way a fin with unwanted hi could never do.

Yondan (four-step) Kohaku. Rarely are the pattern elements this clear-cut.

Above: This koi combines the zig-zag Inazuma (lightning strike) pattern with a Maruten head pattern and is therefore technically a Nidan (two-step) Kohaku.

111

KOHAKU

through later life as its skin stretches, whereas a youngster with apparently over-heavy hi is more likely to 'grow into itself' as areas of hi separate away from one another.

Hi extending below the lateral line is not a fault, but it is better if it does not intrude into any of the fins. Ideally, in all Kohaku there should be an area of white separating the caudal peduncle from the hindmost hi step (ojime). But a tail region lacking any hi is a worse fault, as it unbalances the koi's overall appearance. Watch out, too, for pale and unstable secondary hi (nibani), a mark of poor-quality fish, or pale 'windows', which may indicate that the Kohaku is in the process of losing its hi altogether.

Provided it forms an interesting pattern, unbroken hi running from the head towards the tail is quite acceptable. The best example is the Inazuma (lightning strike), where the red traces a more or less zigzag path across the back. However, Ippon hi (unrelieved hi all over the back and flanks) is not the mark of a good Kohaku and fish like this are usually culled early in life. Other non-starters in Kohaku

Lipstick lib

The Japanese used to be uneasy about Kuchibeni 'lipstick' markings on koi. They were a reminder of the heavy make-up used by Geisha girls, and therefore not respectable. However, in the West, such markings are seen as charming and cute, as well as serving to balance head patterns that stop well short of the koi's nose. Accordingly, breeders are meeting the demand for more koi of this type.

Tail break

One of the old judging standards for Kohaku still holds good: the need for a break between the hindmost area of hi and the wrist of the tail (the caudal peduncle). This 'ojime' balances the white nose and contains the hi pattern. However, it is true to say that today, all rules are there to be broken.

broods are Shiro Muji (all-white koi) and their opposite numbers, the all-red Aka Muji.

Head hi takes many forms. The ideal used to be a bold U-shape, centrally placed and extending level with the eyes, but never running into them. Now, though, the trend is towards Kohaku that 'break the rules' in a novel way. As long as the head pattern is interesting and complements the body hi, almost anything goes. In fact, fish like this tend to win shows because they stand out from the more traditionally patterned koi.

Red lips are known as Kuchibeni (lipstick). They can counterpoint head hi that might otherwise seem uninteresting or sparse.

A fish with stand-alone head hi (quite separate from that on the body) is known as a Maruten Kohaku. This marking counts as a step pattern.

Hi is always more clear-cut on the scaleless head than elsewhere on the fish. Sashi (where white scales overlay hi at the front end of the pattern) is never as clear-cut as kiwa (where red scales overlay white), but should be as sharp as possible. The hi of mature koi should be strong enough to disguise individual

Fore and aft

*Because white scales always overlay red (sashi)
to the fore of a pattern, Kohaku hi is never as
clearly delineated here as it is to the rear (kiwa).
As the hi thickens, the effect becomes less
pronounced. It applies only to fully scaled koi,
including Gin-Rin Kohaku and all other
patterned varieties.*

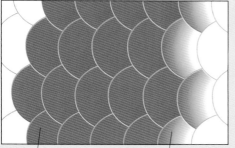

Kiwa, where red
scales overlay
white.

Sashi, where
white scales
overlay red.

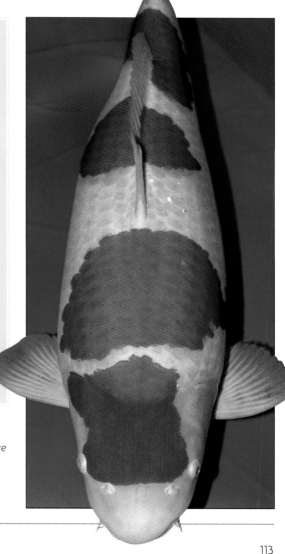

Right: *Clear-cut sashi (to the fore
of each pattern step) combines
with wonderful skin and body
shape in a mature Yondan
(four-step) Maruten Kohaku.*

113

KOHAKU

scales, but thin hi (kokesuke) will often deepen with age in Kohaku of good bloodline.

Doitsu, Gin-Rin, Metallic and other Kohaku

Doitsu Kohaku lack overall scaling. They make attractive, clear-cut pond fish, but in shows without a separate Doitsu class, all other attributes being equal, they will always lose out to fully scaled fish.

Gin-Rin Kohaku, with an abundance of reflective scales, join the other Go Sanke (Sanke and Showa) in their own judging class, Kin-Gin-Rin.

Metallic Kohaku (or Sakura Ogon) are judged in Hikarimoyo.

So-called 'Kanoko Kohaku' have dappled hi made up of clearly defined individual red scales. These fish often lose all their hi later in life, but where it is stable they are judged in Kawarimono.

Head hi

Formal standards for Kohaku head markings have given way to a realisation that unique patterns are equally valid. These are three examples of fish that would certainly catch a judge's eye.

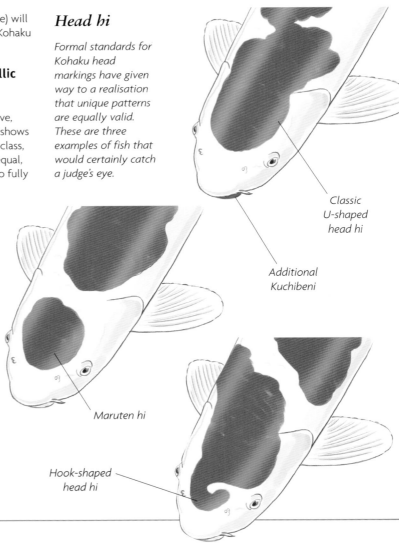

Classic U-shaped head hi

Additional Kuchibeni

Maruten hi

Hook-shaped head hi

Ojime (a white caudal peduncle) relieves the hindmost hi pattern.

Charming, symmetrical hi, bisected by a pure white dorsal fin.

Right: Gin-Rin Kohaku are benched Kin-Gin-Rin in the West. This example fulfils all the criteria for a good Kohaku, even before taking into account its covering of reflective scales. Gin-Rin should enhance merits, rather than conceal faults.

Right: The pattern of this Doitsu Kohaku leads the eye right down the body of the fish; it is almost maplike over the head and shoulders. Impeccable white skin is just as important on Doitsu as it is on fully scaled fish.

115

SANKE

Sanke are koi that combine the red-on-white Kohaku pattern with the added element of sumi (black). When three, rather than two, colours interact there are many possible permutations – some bold and brash, others much more subtle. Hence Sanke work at all levels, appealing just as much to people who simply want attractive pond fish as to those whose aim is to win shows. As part of the Go Sanke triumvirate – the others being Kohaku and Showa – Sanke are highly esteemed in Japan, and no effort is being spared to refine and improve the variety.

The first Sanke

When recognisable Sanke first appeared is debatable, but tricoloured koi were probably around by the end of the nineteenth century. The old name 'Taisho Sanshoku' would place them in the period 1912-1926, and certainly the present-day bloodlines began when white fish with red and black markings appeared spontaneously in 1914 in a brood of Kohaku. Another breeder crossed the parent Kohaku with a Shiro Bekko (a white koi with black Sanke-type markings), and one of the next-generation female offspring was run with a male Yagozen (bloodline name) Kohaku. The resulting Torazo bloodline, and an unrelated strain which has since died out, together form the genetic building blocks of Sanke today. Modern bloodlines include Jinbei, Sadazo, Kichinai and Matsunosuke.

Sanke patterns

Because Sanke are so closely linked with Kohaku, it is not surprising that the starting point for a good specimen is that it shows a credible Kohaku pattern. In other words, try to ignore the sumi and concentrate on the hi, which should be interestingly placed and strong in its own right. Although we do not speak of Nidan, Sandan or Yondan

Left: *This Sanke has many unique features. Crown-shaped head hi, semicircular shoulder sumi and pleasing overall pattern are complemented by superb white skin.*

Right: *The hi pattern on the head of this Sanke is bold without being overwhelming, and the cut of the white into the shoulder contrasts with the sumi to the right. Sanke do not usually have sumi on the head.*

Well-shaped, pure white pectoral fins. Sumi stripes are not essential in Sanke.

SANKE

(step-patterned) Sanke, Kohaku-type block patterns are a feature of many of these koi. Sumi should not 'fill in' for deficiencies in hi distribution. The black is a complementary colour.

Choosing Sanke

Buying young high-grade Sanke can be exciting, not to say risky. Many of the best examples show little, if any, sumi until the age of two. Outwardly, they are Kohaku. Only the breeder can make an educated guess, from past experience, as to how these koi will develop, because the various bloodlines perform in very different ways. For example, Matsunosuke Sanke start life with very faint, blue-grey sumi that

gradually deepens, whereas Kichinai Sanke appear 'finished' at an early age. Here, the only real change is that the skin stretches as it grows, affecting the distribution of hi and sumi over the white base colour. For that reason, young Sanke that are perfect miniatures of mature koi are not always a wise buy, although they may initially do well in shows. Sanke sumi in yearling koi may even vanish in the second season and reappear later. Early, stable sumi is called 'moto sumi', while black that appears later is known as 'ato sumi'. Sumi can overlay either hi (kasane sumi) or white skin (tsubo sumi). In most Sanke, both types are present, but those rare koi displaying only tsubo sumi are especially sought after. However, this

Sanke trademarks

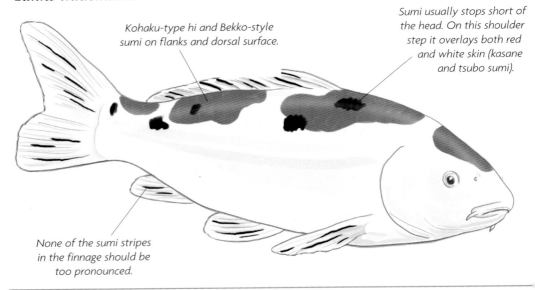

Kohaku-type hi and Bekko-style sumi on flanks and dorsal surface.

Sumi usually stops short of the head. On this shoulder step it overlays both red and white skin (kasane and tsubo sumi).

None of the sumi stripes in the finnage should be too pronounced.

Future champions

Tategoi Sanke are quality fish with potential to improve further. Hi may be thin, sumi sparse and body shape uninteresting, but good skin quality is non-negotiable; without it, the koi will never be more than a pretty pond fish. With Tategoi you buy a dream that may or may not become reality.

Right: *Pattern and skin quality already mark out this Tategoi Sanke as special. As more sumi emerges, the fish will become still more desirable.*

Revealing pecs

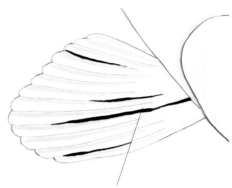

If present on Sanke pectoral fins, sumi takes the form of stripes.

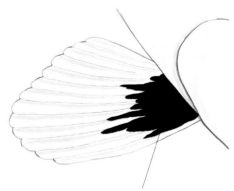

On Showa, pectoral sumi is typically concentrated in the ball joint of the fin (motoguro).

SANKE

situation may change, because tastes in Sanke are subject to fashion. Once, heavy sumi was in vogue. This gave way to a preference for minimalist sumi, present as strategically placed black accents. Now, almost anything goes, as long as the overall effect is pleasing. As with Kohaku, individuals that creatively break the rules and appear 'unique' tend to score over fish with more traditional patterns.

Certain ground rules, or Sanke 'trademarks', help distinguish them from the superficially similar Showa. Sanke sumi is of the Bekko, or tortoiseshell type, and rarely present below the lateral line or on the head. It may or may not extend into the finnage. If it does, the pectoral sumi typically takes the form of subtle stripes, rather than an aggregation of black in the ball joint area with stripes radiating from it – known in Showa as 'motoguro'. Nevertheless it is becoming ever harder to tell the two varieties apart, and no single 'trademark' can be a foolproof guide to identification. Only by evaluating them all together does the picture become clearer.

Sanke varieties

Tancho Sanke are effectively Shiro Bekko with additional hi confined to the head. These are benched Tancho. In Budo Sanke, all the hi is overlaid with sumi, to give a purplish effect. These fish are benched Kawarimono or Koromo. Otherwise, all matt-scaled Sanke are judged in their own class, and the terminology applied to them merely reflects the koi's appearance. For example, in Aka Sanke, hi is the dominant colour. Fish whose pattern runs unrelieved from head to tail, with no interesting white cut-ins, are not well thought of. Unsubtle as they are, good examples of Aka Sanke can still look very imposing.

Below: A Doitsu Maruten Sanke with heavy, well-placed sumi. It could be mistaken for a Showa, but closer inspection reveals white, not black, to be the primary skin colour.

Right: On this mature Maruten Sanke, the head hi is just right, framed all round by snow-white skin.

Like their Kohaku counterparts, Maruten Sanke, have a patch of head hi not connected to the red markings on the body.

'Menkaburi' (meaning 'hood') is the term for head hi extending down over the nose and jaws, while Kuchibeni Sanke have the characteristic lipstick-like hi markings.

Gin-Rin Sanke display numerous sparkling scales; they appear gold over hi and silver over white skin. These koi are benched Gin-Rin, but can be confused with Sanke of the Matsunosuke bloodline, whose skin has a subtle shine termed 'fukurin'. There is an ongoing debate as to whether this term should apply to Go Sanke at all, but meanwhile these Matsunosuke fish continue to be benched Sanke, not Gin-Rin. A further refinement of Matsunosuke Sanke is that the bloodline has been back-crossed with ancestral Magoi to improve growth potential. Young fish, therefore, tend to be slimmer than most other koi, taking several years to attain a voluminous body shape.

There is no identity crisis with Doitsu Sanke. These are very sharply dressed koi, with no scales to blur the pattern edges. Good examples look as though the colours have been applied thickly with a brush. In most Western shows they are benched with other Sanke, and fare poorly against them because they lack subtlety. However, in shows run along Japanese lines, they go into a separate Doitsu judging class, where they do not have to compete against fully scaled koi.

Metallic Sanke (Yamatonishiki) are benched Hikarimoyo, and all crosses between Sanke and other, non-metallic koi (except Koromo) go into the catch-all Kawarimono class.

SHOWA

Showa share an unlikely quality with polar bears – they both have black skin. In the bear this is hidden by thick white fur, while in the koi the sumi pigment may not always dominate. Nonetheless, Showa are always black fish with red and white markings. This distinguishes them from Sanke, which have white skin.

The first Showa

Of the three koi varieties collectively known as Go Sanke, Showa are by far the youngest. They can be traced back to 1927, when a breeder in Niigata crossed a Ki Utsuri (a black fish with yellow markings) with a Kohaku. As you might expect, this produced tricolour koi in which the hi was a washed-out orange. Only in 1965, when descendants of these early Showa were back-crossed to Sanke and other Kohaku, did proper scarlet hi and deep, glossy sumi begin to appear.

Showa do not have directly traceable bloodlines, and the continued introduction of Sanke genes is blurring the distinctions between the two varieties. The configuration, rather than the amount, of sumi remains the benchmark. In traditional Showa, where red is the predominant colour, the black takes the form of bold wrappings, sometimes extending up from the belly, and quite different to typical Sanke 'tortoiseshell' sumi of the Bekko type, which is confined to the area above the lateral line.

Showa signatures

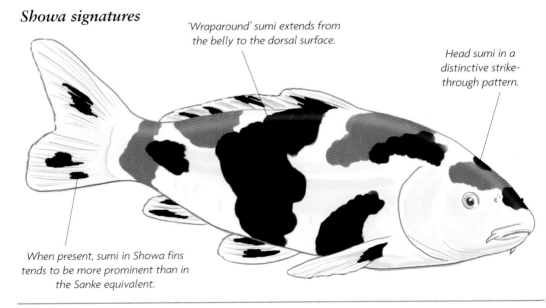

'Wraparound' sumi extends from the belly to the dorsal surface.

Head sumi in a distinctive strike-through pattern.

When present, sumi in Showa fins tends to be more prominent than in the Sanke equivalent.

Below: *A Hi (predominantly red) Showa. This one, although Tategoi, already shows classic menware head sumi and even motoguro in the pectoral fins. Sumi below the dorsal fin is still unfinished.*

Showa patterns

Even on Kindai Showa – which, with their blinding white skin, seem at first glance to be more like Sanke – the sumi is the giveaway. It is nearly always present on the head, striking through the hi and white. 'Menware' sumi resembles a lightning bolt, while another well-known Showa head sumi configuration is V-shaped, starting on the shoulders, with the pointed end towards the nose. However, there is no set standard for Showa head markings. The important thing is that they are attractive: all-black heads, or smudged sumi, are not.

The Showa equivalent of an Aka Sanke is a Hi Showa (both 'aka' and 'hi' meaning red). But because Showa sumi is so bold and distinctive, it can lift the overall appearance of the koi, even when there is little white present. Hi Showa are easily confused with Hi Utsuri, which are black koi with exclusively red markings. If any white at all is visible on the body when the fish is viewed at a 45° angle, the koi is still Showa.

The ideal motoguro pattern on Showa pectoral fins consists of evenly matched semicircular blocks of sumi around the ball joints. These may be present in very young fish, or may develop through shrinkage of pigment in fins that start off all black. On the other hand, dark fins may remain that way. If they do, both left and right pectorals should mirror one another, otherwise the Showa will look unbalanced.

There is generally more sumi in Showa than in Sanke finnage although, again, some Kindai (predominantly white) Showa may show none at all.

SHOWA

Changing faces

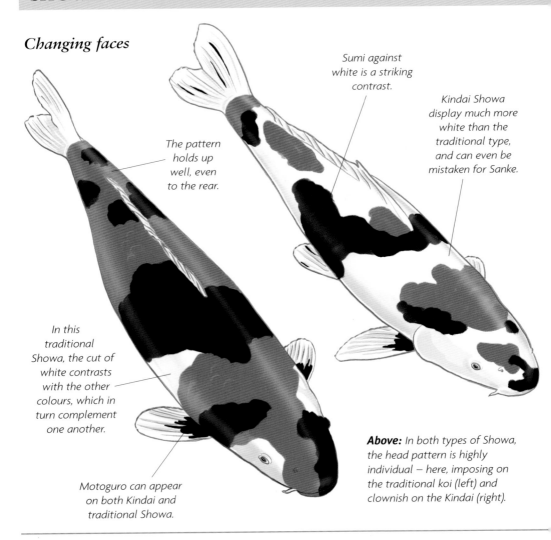

Sumi against white is a striking contrast.

Kindai Showa display much more white than the traditional type, and can even be mistaken for Sanke.

The pattern holds up well, even to the rear.

In this traditional Showa, the cut of white contrasts with the other colours, which in turn complement one another.

Motoguro can appear on both Kindai and traditional Showa.

Above: In both types of Showa, the head pattern is highly individual – here, imposing on the traditional koi (left) and clownish on the Kindai (right).

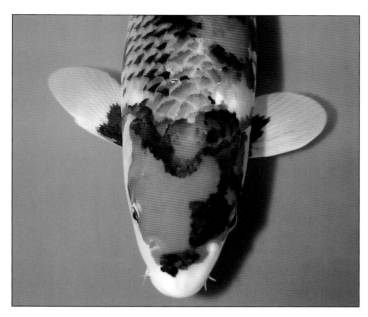

Left: On this mature Showa, the kage sumi may by now be stabilised. As Kage Showa are not benched separately in the West, it is academic what this koi is called – opinions will vary.

Below: This Hi Showa shows both glossy black finished sumi and shadowy kage sumi just in front and to the side of the dorsal fin. Whether or not this fills in later, the fish has too much traditional sumi to be classed as a Kage Hi Showa.

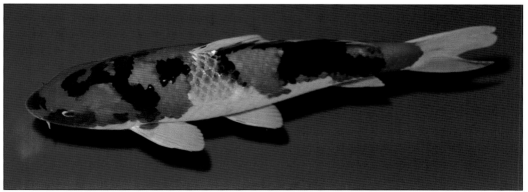

SHOWA

Choosing Showa

More than any other koi variety, Showa are prone to physical deformities of the mouth and spine. If these are obvious, steer clear of the fish. More often, the defects are not that clear-cut and become apparent only on close inspection. View the koi from all angles, note how it swims, and give it a thorough looking over when it is first bagged up.

Another common failing is seen in Showa whose front-end patterning tails away to virtually nothing. Because the interaction of three colours is so successful, it is easy to be beguiled by a charming head, while failing to notice that the tail end of the fish lacks hi, or else is sumi-heavy.

Fully emerged Showa sumi should be a deep, glossy black, with no hint of chocolate brown. Hard water, rich in calcium and magnesium salts, brings out black better than soft water. Emergent sumi is blue-grey, and forms a netlike pattern under the skin, which fills in with age. On some fish this dappled, shadowy sumi remains into adulthood, and the koi are then described as Kage Showa. In the West these were once benched Kawarimono, which led to disputes between owners and judges, because the distinction between finished and unfinished sumi is difficult to draw.

Showa varieties

No variety changes so radically with age as Showa. Babies can resemble Kohaku or Sanke, with only a hint of sumi. Hi markings, too, can come and go before they stabilise. This makes Showa a very

Left: A bright and beautiful Gin-Rin Kindai Showa. Tail-end sumi may yet become over-heavy, whereas that on the head still has some way to go. An exciting prospect.

The striped pectoral fins merely enhance the overall effect.

exciting prospect, as even the breeders cannot tell with any certainty how pattern will develop. It may get better, it may get worse. So if you buy a young fish with good body shape and skin quality, its potential lies in the lap of the gods, to be maximised by good koi-keeping practice.

Tancho Showa are benched Tancho. Unlike in their Sanke counterparts, the head hi marking is usually struck through with sumi, rather than standing alone.

Gin-Rin Showa (benched Gin-Rin) are not very common in the West, but deserve to be: good examples practically glow. As in all Gin-Rin koi, the presence of sparkling scales should not blind you to obvious shortfalls in pattern or skin quality. Similarly, the white skin of Doitsu Showa must be the colour of snow, with no hint of a bluish tinge, and the enlarged scales along the dorsal surface and flanks need to be evenly arranged.

Some noteworthy Showa crosses include Koromo Showa, with interesting reticulation of the hi (benched Showa), and Showa Shusui (Doitsu fish where the dorsal scales are blue). These go into the Kawarimono class.

Left: *The saddle of white towards the tail of this Doitsu Showa, and more white on the head and shoulders, does not entirely relieve what some observers would regard as an oppressive pattern.*

UTSURIMONO

The vagaries of fashion in koi-keeping are well demonstrated by changing tastes in black-and-white fish. Shiro Bekko – white koi with Sanke-style sumi – have fallen from public favour, if show entries are any yardstick, whereas the superficially similar Shiro Utsuri has achieved a status only a little below that of Kohaku, Sanke and Showa. This may be because the pattern is altogether bolder and, as a stand-alone feature, more interesting and variable than in Bekko, where the emphasis is on subtle understatement.

Shiro Utsuri are benched Utsurimono, a classification in which three varieties share the same type of sumi (black) – the primary skin colour. The others are Hi Utsuri (red on black) and Ki Utsuri (yellow on black). Although the latter was instrumental in the development of Showa, it is a variety seldom seen today, although its metallic equivalent, the Kin Ki Utsuri, is still common.

Shiro Utsuri are variously credited with direct Magoi antecedents or as being of more recent Showa descent. The sumi is certainly of the wraparound type, and in any Showa spawning there will always be fish lacking hi. Nowadays, however, Shiro Utsuri are so highly valued that 'accidental' examples are far outnumbered by fish bred from parents of that variety. As in Sanke and Kindai Showa, the preference for large amounts of sumi has given way to one for brighter fish in which the white predominates – although Shiro Utsuri of the original type are still valued, too.

Developing patterns

Looking at young fish, it is difficult to predict how the pattern will develop. Many of the best Tategoi Shiro Utsuri start life with only shadowy sumi markings that appear blue-grey under the skin. The best guideline is the koi's parentage, and whether fish from a given breeder tend towards light or heavy markings in adulthood.

Above: *This Tategoi Shiro Utsuri already displays wonderful skin quality and sparse, though still-developing, sumi. Compare this with the mature fish pictured at right, which has a fully finished pattern and more voluminous body shape.*

Fin distinctions

Classic Shiro Utsuri pectoral fins show a sumi pattern known as 'motoguro', where the black forms a solid block around the ball joint. In Sanke, the equivalent pattern is made up of separated individual stripes following the fin rays. But as Sanke, Showa and Shiro Utsuri are interbred, intermediate pectoral sumi is becoming more common. All-black pectorals in Shiro Utsuri are a definite demerit, although the sumi may retreat as the fish matures.

Intermediate Shiro Utsuri sumi, where the black radiates outwards from the usual motoguro.

Left: This head study of a Shiro Utsuri reveals the sumi to be of Showa type – wrapping around the body and travelling down the face as befits the primary skin colour. The white lips offer a pleasing counterpoint.

UTSURIMONO

Skin, too, can be deceptive in the early months, with a bluish tone and sometimes a yellowish tinge to the head, where there are no scales. This usually turns white as the skull bones and the skin covering them thicken. The wrist of the tail is where you will see the first indication of the final white ground colour and, all other things being equal, you should select the fish with the palest caudal peduncles. After that, it is down to part luck, part good water management. Hard, alkaline water brings out sumi to a finished deep, glossy black, although sumi of inferior Shiro Utsuri, on close inspection in good light, is more of a chocolate brown.

Head sumi, which may take years to emerge fully, is comparable to that of Showa, and may take either the traditional menware path or be more sparing and subtle. Excessively heavy head markings, or an over-fussy pattern on the face, will detract from the koi's appearance. Pattern symmetry is not important, but overall balance is. Too much, or not enough, sumi in the tail region is a common fault.

An otherwise excellent Shiro Utsuri can be ruined by its finnage. Some sumi is permitted on the dorsal, tail and undercarriage fins, but the pectorals should ideally resemble those of a Showa – either the classic matching motoguro markings around the ball joint or no sumi at all. All-black pectoral fins may later form motoguro; the worst pairing is black one side, white the other, especially if the fins do not contrast with the adjacent body colour.

Choosing Shiro Utsuri

Shiro Utsuri breed relatively true to variety, so good examples are far outnumbered by ordinary-grade fish whose body shape lets them down. When choosing from a number of youngsters, go for those with thick shoulders and caudal peduncle, refusing any that appear pinched-in behind the gill covers or have long, pointed heads.

In Gin-Rin Shiro Utsuri, the reflective scales show silver over both white skin and sumi, and the koi look very chic and not at all flashy. As with all Gin-Rin koi, the trick is to look beneath superficial finery and see if the fish stands up to scrutiny as a good representative of its variety. In the West, Gin-Rin Shiro Utsuri remain in the Utsurimono class,

Heads and shoulders

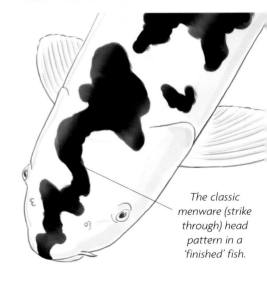

The classic menware (strike through) head pattern in a 'finished' fish.

benched alongside conventionally scaled fish. To succeed against them they need to be not just good, but special.

Doitsu Shiro Utsuri could be confused with Kumonryu, and certainly the head markings are similar. Both are black-and-white, German-scaled fish, but Kumonryu patterning runs from head to tail, quite different from Utsuri-style wrapping.

Hi Utsuri (black koi with red or orange markings) are essentially Showa minus the white and, as in Showa, the quality of the hi has been improved by

outcrossings to Kohaku. There may even be Magoi genes present, to improve growth potential. Hi Utsuri pectoral fins rarely show motoguro, tending to be candy-striped black-and-red, with a red leading edge. It can be difficult to tell this variety from Hi Showa, but the latter always exhibit some white when viewed in the water, something Hi Utsuri never do.

Ki Utsuri, known until the early twentieth century as Kuro-Ki-Han, first appeared in 1875. The variety was stabilised and renamed by Eizaburo Hoshino, the

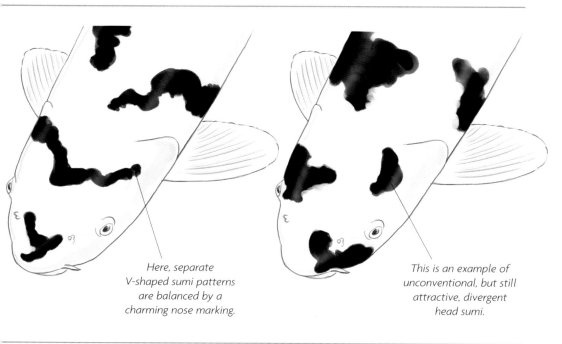

Here, separate V-shaped sumi patterns are balanced by a charming nose marking.

This is an example of unconventional, but still attractive, divergent head sumi.

UTSURIMONO

same man who helped to develop modern Sanke bloodlines, but these days it is seldom seen. There are far more colourful yellow koi to choose from, without such a tendency to disfiguring 'shimis' – and buying a rare koi is no passport to show success, when it is unlikely that there will be others of its type present for comparison.

The history of Utsurimono

The origin of Utsurimono is unclear. Some authorities claim that the fish are of Magoi lineage, first produced in 1925 by Kazuo Minemura. Others maintain that they are of much more recent Showa descent. Both theories are hard to disprove; all koi originate from Magoi, and a Shiro Utsuri could be viewed, unkindly, as a defective Showa without the hi, just as a Shiro Bekko is basically a Sanke lacking a third colour. Nowadays, however, Shiro Utsuri parent koi are spawned together to produce this specific variety, and only a few arise unwanted from Showa spawnings.

Right: One of the cleanest-cut koi possible is a Doitsu Shiro Utsuri. This one follows the modern trend of having predominantly white skin, although more sumi will probably emerge later, as this is still a young fish.

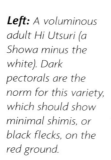

Left: A voluminous adult Hi Utsuri (a Showa minus the white). Dark pectorals are the norm for this variety, which should show minimal shimis, or black flecks, on the red ground.

BEKKO

An alternative name for koi is 'nishikigoi', meaning 'brocaded carp'. The pattern and scalation on some varieties does indeed form a rich tapestry, and to regard koi as living works of art is not to overstate the case.

The coming of Gin-Rin and metallic varieties has added new dimensions to this visual feast. Sometimes they enhance the overall effect. For example, a Gin-Rin Kohaku is none the worse for its coat of glittering scales – as long as the skin and pattern are of top quality. However, a metallic lustre may simply overcrowd and confuse the senses, and rather than improving the appearance of the koi may actually detract from it. This explains why metallic Ai Goromo (Shochikubai) and metallic Sanke (Yamatonishiki) are not as popular as the matt-scaled originals. Light passing through reflective pigment dulls the colours, making red appear orange and black more of a grey.

At the other end of the scale are koi varieties whose simplicity works against them. This is certainly true of the group benched Bekko. Although they retain their own classification, they are an ever-rarer presence at shows. Shiro Bekko (matt-scaled white koi with tortoiseshell sumi) are merely Sanke minus the hi. The best examples are chic and understated, but given the choice, most people would opt for Sanke, where a third colour presents so much more scope for individual excellence.

Before the production of Sanke (and Kindai Showa) with a high percentage of white skin, Shiro Bekko would be introduced to counterpoint other koi in a collection.

Ponds in which one colour predominates never look as pleasing as those where fish are chosen, at least in part, for their contribution to the appearance of the group as a whole.

The white dorsal fin sets of the hi ground colour well, and does not diminish this koi's status as a true Aka Bekko.

Despite a little white on the lips, this fish is an Aka Bekko rather than an Aka Sanke.

Both this Shiro Bekko and the Aka Bekko (above) have the desirable break between sumi and caudal peduncle.

Bekko sumi is always of Sanke, rather than Showa, type. This applies to finnage as well as to the body.

Above: Clear heads are evident in both Aka (top) and Shiro Bekko. Looking at these examples, it is easy to see how both could be thrown from a Sanke spawning: one lacks the white, the other the hi, of a tricoloured fish.

The fashion for Bekko

Certain koi varieties are subject to the vagaries of fashion, first enjoying spells of popularity and then fading from favour. Bekko are a case in point. When koi-keeping began to take off outside Japan about 30 years ago, these fish were very much in vogue; indeed, they were given (and still have) their own benching classification. However, Bekko today are under-represented at most shows. This is a pity, as good specimens are as appealing as ever, in a chic and understated way.

Shiro Bekko, still produced from parent fish of this variety, are just as likely to be thrown from Sanke spawnings. However, if there is any residual hi, they are merely inferior Sanke, and valueless for showing. Israeli-bred Bekko are on a par with those from Japan. They present a unique opportunity to own high-quality fish for a relatively low outlay.

Even ten years ago, acceptable Shiro Bekko sumi would be relatively heavy, in line with that of Sanke of the period. Nowadays, 'less is more'. The sumi, always confined to the area above the lateral line, can be extremely sparse, serving only to highlight a snow-white skin with a high lustre. A little sumi on the head is permissible, but the best examples still have a clear white face to show off their blue eyes. The heads of young Shiro Bekko are often yellowish, a colour that may fail to clear to white with age.

BEKKO

Sumi patterning should balance overall, and not be confined to one side of the fish. As in Kohaku, an area of white at the junction of body and tail fin is desirable – too much black at the rear end takes the eye in the wrong direction. Shiro Bekko pectoral finnage can be either clear white or striped with sumi, Sanke-style.

Aka Bekko are red koi with sumi markings – rare but striking. They are easily confused with Aka Sanke, which show a little white when viewed from above. The pectoral fins can be any combination of red and white, with or without sumi striping.

Ki Bekko (yellow fish with black markings) are the rarest in this group. Nowadays they are not deliberately spawned, but arise from Shiro Bekko x Kigoi or Sanke x Kigoi crosses. The commoner, metallic equivalent is the Toro (Tiger) Ogon.

Doitsu and Gin-Rin Shiro Bekko (both benched Bekko in the West) can be striking koi. The dorsal mirror scales of the Doitsu

Right: *A near-perfect Gin-Rin Bekko – clear head, understated but well-positioned sumi and a beautiful ground colour enhanced by shimmering reflective scales. The pectoral fins are especially impressive, with their sumi stripes that mark this fish down as a Sanke variant.*

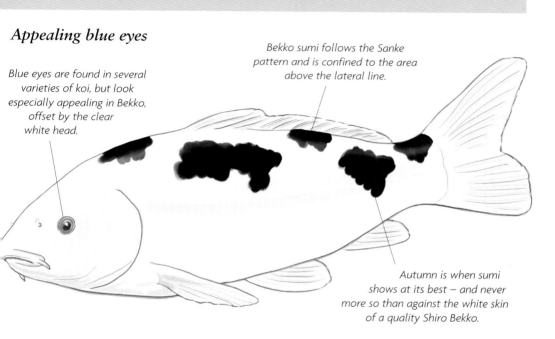

Appealing blue eyes

Blue eyes are found in several varieties of koi, but look especially appealing in Bekko, offset by the clear white head.

Bekko sumi follows the Sanke pattern and is confined to the area above the lateral line.

Autumn is when sumi shows at its best – and never more so than against the white skin of a quality Shiro Bekko.

Bekko are silvery white, contrasting beautifully with any sumi they overlay, while Gin-Rin scalation enhances the subtle attributes of what can otherwise be an understated, and undervalued, variety.

Since Shiro Bekko are Sanke lacking hi, the sumi will follow the same developmental process as in the tri-coloured fish – in other words, it can emerge and stabilise early in life, or fade and then reappear. It all depends on the bloodline. However, there are other dark markings, called shimis, which can spoil koi of all varieties. These individual dark scales appear on the ground colour and detract from the 'clean' appearance of the fish. Poor diet and water conditions, or simply advancing age, may be responsible for shimis: when they are found on a Shiro Bekko it is easy to appreciate the difference between these and true sumi. The presence of one or two blemishes is unfortunate, but permissible – it is when shimis appear on koi varieties with no black in their pattern, such as Kohaku, that they constitute a disaster for showing purposes! Sometimes, the pigment can be scraped from rogue scales with a fingernail; otherwise, leave well alone.

ASAGI AND SHUSUI

Asagi play a central role in the history of koi, as all other varieties have been developed from these fully scaled, non-metallic fish. How much interest they still generate can be judged only on present-day demand which, in the West at least, is on the decline.

Asagi closely resemble Asagi Magoi, of which there are two variants. The dark Konjo Asagi, bred as food fish, played a part in the development of Matsubagoi. Narumi Asagi, suitably refined, are the direct descendants of mutant fish named for their supposed resemblance to a blue fabric made in that town in Northern Japan. They had a blue reticulated back, and rusty red hi on the cheeks, flanks and pectoral fins. Leaving aside heightened colours and more evenly distributed hi, this description holds good for today's Asagi.

Ordinary-grade Asagi are easy to produce and uninspiring to look at, but nobody should dismiss this variety until they have seen a few prizewinning examples. The back should be evenly covered in pale blue scales with a darker outer edging. A sharp demarcation between the two shades produces the desired reticulation. With age, the skin stretches and this 'true fukurin' effect becomes yet more pronounced. The head should ideally be pure white, but is more likely to be grey or bluish, with spot blemishes of hi. Larger hi markings on the jaw and cheeks are no fault, while if head hi forms a hoodlike pattern the fish is known as a Menkaburi Asagi.

On the body, hi runs up from the belly to the lateral line or beyond, although in low-grade Asagi hi can be absent altogether and the fish are a uniform blue. Pectoral fin hi is either configured like the motoguro of Showa (see page 123) or covers the fins entirely – the important thing is that it matches left and right.

Asagi with red markings reaching up almost to the dorsal surface are known as Hi Asagi. Taki Sanke (still Asagi, despite the name) have a white line separating areas of red and blue on the flanks.

Hi Asagi and Taki Sanke

In Hi Asagi, red intrudes well into the reticulated blue ground colour.

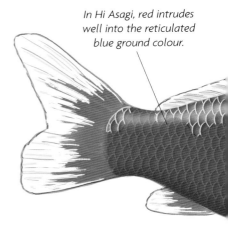

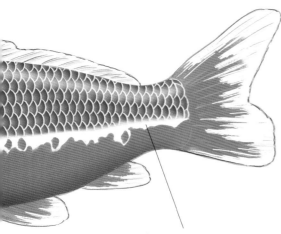

Below: *The head on this classic Asagi is particularly attractive, with even cheek hi and a symmetrical nose spot on an otherwise clear white ground. In fact, everything about this koi is balanced, even the pectoral finnage.*

In Taki Sanke, a white flank stripe separates the blue back and red belly.

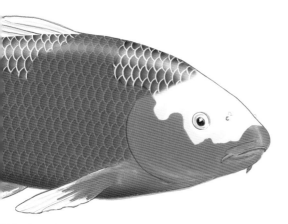

ASAGI AND SHUSUI

Left: This Asagi is hard to fault. The deep blue back shows even reticulation, the head is almost blemish-free, and the body is filled out without being fat. Note the demarcation between scaled body and scaleless head.

Right: Hi and conventional Asagi demonstrate the variability of this very old koi variety. If the fish on the left were metallic, it would be a very acceptable Kujaku. The hi over blue does not obscure the necessary scale reticulation. In the fish to the right, blue is the dominant colour. Ideally, its head should be clearer than it is.

ASAGI AND SHUSUI

Shusui

Asagi belong in the same show classification as their Doitsu counterparts, Shusui – meaning 'Autumn water'. Shusui arose in about 1910 from crosses between Asagi and German carp with enlarged mirrorlike scales confined to the dorsal surface and lateral lines. This feature made them easier to clean for the table. Instead of a reticulated pattern, the smooth, sky-blue back is highlighted by this 'Doitsu' (German) scalation, which should form a regular pattern on the shoulders and run in two lines either side of the dorsal, reducing to a single line on the caudal peduncle. Other enlarged scales may follow the path of the lateral line.

On Hi Shusui, the red extends up over the back, complementing the dark blue Doitsu scales. Hana Shusui, too, have more red than normal, this time as an extra wavy-edged band between the lateral line and dorsal fin.

In Ki Shusui, yellow replaces the red. If the dorsal scales are black or greyish, this subvariety is easy to confuse with a Doitsu Ki Matsuba. (The greenish yellow Midorigoi, which is benched in Kawarimono, is also very Shusui-like.)

Shusui crosses include Showa Shusui, Sanke Shusui and Goshiki Shusui. These koi show characteristics of both parents, but with ice-blue, rather than white, skin. They are benched Kawarimono. Shusui crossed with metallic Ogons result in Ginsui and Kinsui, which are rarely seen today.

When choosing Shusui, watch out for messy or asymmetrical shoulder scale patterns, or individual rogue scales appearing anywhere on the body – particularly the belly. A clear head is an essential requisite. In hard water, the mirror scales can turn greyish or black, and once this happens they never revert back to blue. Shusui are also prone to shimis and middle-aged spread, so to grow on a fish that retains a good shape and clear colours is quite an achievement.

Above: Hi or Hana Shusui? It won't affect where this koi is judged, but in any event, red is a dominant colour on this attractive fish. Note the break between the dorsal and shoulder scale patterns.

Below: The deep blue Doitsu scales on the dorsal surface of this Shusui set off both the bluish white and red areas of otherwise naked skin, but they could be more evenly aligned.

ASAGI AND SHUSUI

Hi Shusui and Ki Shusui

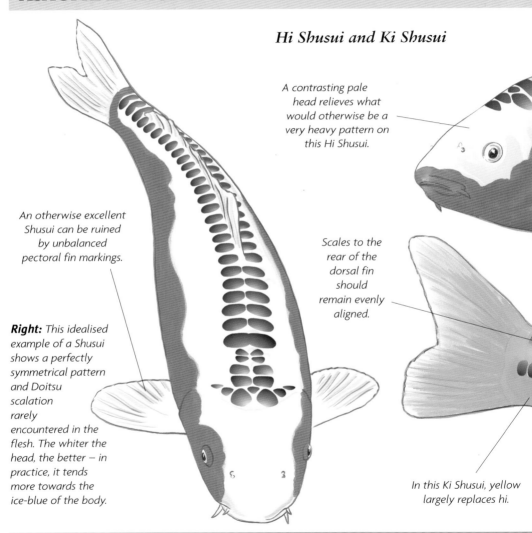

A contrasting pale head relieves what would otherwise be a very heavy pattern on this Hi Shusui.

An otherwise excellent Shusui can be ruined by unbalanced pectoral fin markings.

Scales to the rear of the dorsal fin should remain evenly aligned.

Right: This idealised example of a Shusui shows a perfectly symmetrical pattern and Doitsu scalation rarely encountered in the flesh. The whiter the head, the better – in practice, it tends more towards the ice-blue of the body.

In this Ki Shusui, yellow largely replaces hi.

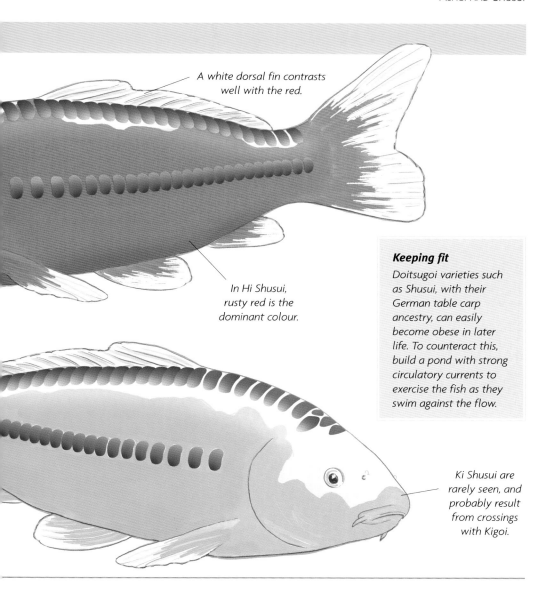

A white dorsal fin contrasts well with the red.

In Hi Shusui, rusty red is the dominant colour.

Keeping fit

Doitsugoi varieties such as Shusui, with their German table carp ancestry, can easily become obese in later life. To counteract this, build a pond with strong circulatory currents to exercise the fish as they swim against the flow.

Ki Shusui are rarely seen, and probably result from crossings with Kigoi.

KOROMO

Koromo are cross-bred koi (hybridisation is another matter, involving parents of different species). Most koi varieties stem from crossings, but in Koromo the parentage is very obvious – Kohaku and Asagi. Koromo is the Japanese word for 'robed', and aptly describes a group of koi that first became available in the 1950s. From the Kohaku side of the family tree comes white skin with a hi pattern, while the Asagi genes contribute black or blue secondary colours to the red areas alone. In the West, the issue is no longer quite so clear-cut, as Goshiki (five-colour koi) are now included in Koromo. In these koi, the pattern overlay intrudes into the white skin. The change in classification was made to avoid show benching disputes in borderline cases.

The classic Koromo is the Ai Goromo, and a good example should display all the qualities expected of a Kohaku – snow-white skin and deep crimson hi. Blue or blue-black scale reticulation may take years to emerge fully over the hi. Whether it then confines itself to these areas, or moves further over the body, determines whether the fish remains an Ai Goromo or becomes a Goshiki. Some individuals are legitimately benched in both varieties at different stages in their lives.

Young high-quality Ai Goromo can appear very Kohaku-like, which is no bad thing. A robed pattern that emerges too early may develop to excess and overwhelm the koi. In mature fish the blue scale centres should be evenly distributed over all patches of hi, with the exception of any present on the head.

Sumi Goromo are white koi with a black pattern, each scale of which is edged in red – a mirror image of what happens in Ai Goromo. Very occasionally, none of this red edging emerges, and we are left with a 'black Kohaku', which would have to be benched Kawarimono.

An Ai Goromo needs a good Kohaku pattern as the base for its 'robing' of blue over hi.

Right: *Young Ai Goromo can look very much like Kohaku for up to three years. This Tategoi has yet to develop full robing, but all the other elements are in place, including superb skin and an interesting Inazuma (lightning strike) pattern.*

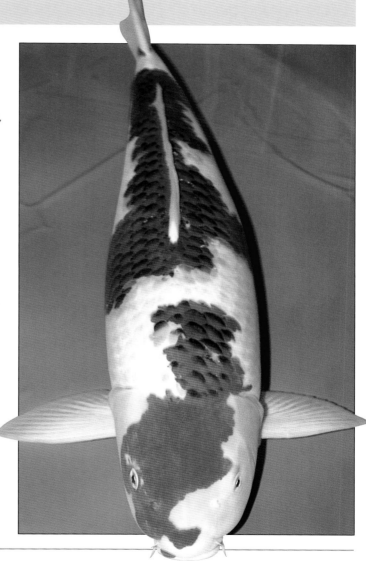

Another definition of a Sumi Goromo is a red-and-white koi in which all areas of hi, including those on the head, are fully overlaid with black. These fish have a quiet elegance but, in truth, dark Ai Goromo and light Sumi Goromo can look very similar.

A Budo Goromo is a Sumi Goromo variant with purplish patches of overlaid hi. Kiwa and sashi show as individual scales picked out against the white, reminiscent of bunches of grapes in shape and colour. The very similar Budo Sanke has sumi overlaying the hi, with additional solid Sanke-type 'Hon' sumi markings. The inference to draw is that they result from Sumi Goromo/Sanke crosses.

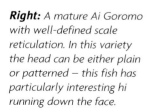

Right: *A mature Ai Goromo with well-defined scale reticulation. In this variety the head can be either plain or patterned – this fish has particularly interesting hi running down the face.*

KOROMO

Something for everyone

Within the Goshiki variety are fish so diverse in appearance that beginners to koi-keeping would never dream they are grouped together. At one extreme are dark, rather muddy-looking koi; at the other, fish with superb pattern definition, plenty of clear white skin and real 'presence'. Modern Goshiki are right up among Go Sanke in terms of koi that can be appreciated at several levels, and the best examples command high prices.

Left: *In Budo Goromo, the form the pattern takes defines the variety just as much as its colours; the combined elements are said to resemble bunches of grapes. The pure white head here offers a startling contrast.*

Right: *A mature three-step Sumi Goromo has an almost maplike pattern around the dorsal fin. Scale reticulation is less pronounced than on an Ai Goromo, as sumi fully overlays the hi.*

Above: This Goshiki is also Gin-Rin, but the sparkling scales only show to good effect because the overall pattern is so superb – even though the fish lacks much white. Pectoral fin hi harks back to Asagi lineage.

KOROMO

Doitsu Ai Goromo are among the rarest of koi. The only blue/black scales are the enlarged ones running along the back. In all other respects the fish is a Doitsu Kohaku, with no intrusion of another colour into the body hi. In the West, all Doitsugoi, with the exception of Go Sanke, are benched under their own variety, so the correct classification of this type of fish is Koromo.

Goshiki, the 'new recruits' to Koromo, are allegedly five-coloured koi – red, black, white, and light and dark blue. The traditional Goshiki is a dark fish with rather indistinct patterning, sometimes relieved by clear patches of hi. Others look like straight Kohaku x Asagi crosses, with a black reticulation over the whole body. A sixth colour, purple, is apparent when sumi overlays blue. Modern Goshiki closely resemble Koromo Showa. By no means all the hi is overlaid, and sometimes fish show reticulation only over the secondary colours. They can be confused at first glance with Kujaku, but these are metallic, not matt, koi. White is the prevailing colour in modern Goshiki, giving these fish a clear-cut look.

In Gin-Rin Goshiki, where the appearance of the reflective scales is determined by the skin tones beneath, almost limitless colour permutations are possible. Doitsu Goshiki, by contrast, are quite subdued. The blue from the Asagi lineage cannot form a reticulated pattern, as there are no scales: instead, blocks of subtle colour characterise these somewhat uncommon fish.

Ai Goromo were derived from Kohaku but have subsequently been crossed with other Go Sanke, with varying success. A Koromo Sanke is essentially an Ai Goromo with Sanke Hon sumi (solid Sanke-type markings) in addition to the blue/black centres to each red scale. In the West, it is benched Koromo.

Showa x Koromo crosses can turn out to be very sophisticated-looking koi. The fact that the hi tends to be brownish red, rather than crimson, does not matter. It serves as a subtle ground colour over which the Hon sumi runs, extending over the head in typical Showa fashion. But all Koromo, these included, must have impeccable white skin.

Below: *For quiet sophistication, a good Koromo Showa is hard to beat. The scale reticulation on this example is confined to the body hi, contrasting with the oblique mask of solid face sumi of Showa derivation.*

Above: *This is a really superb Goshiki. The reticulated and scalloped hi pattern stands out against the milk-white skin, and the head, with blue eyes and a charming nose spot, is beguiling.*

KAWARIMONO

Koi benched Kawarimono are non-metallic fish of named varieties that do not fall within other classifications. This diverse group takes in Doitsu (scaleless) and Gin-Rin (koi with reflective silver scales), as well as fully scaled matt koi, of one or more colours, and includes fish of the Karasu lineage, which are close to the ancestral Magoi.

Also placed in Kawarimono are the true 'one-offs', or unique koi – pleasing, non-metallic crosses whose exact parentage may or may not be apparent.

The Kawarimono class is well represented at shows, due in large measure to the popularity of Chagoi and Kumonryu. Within the group are fish to appeal to all hobbyists, and few ponds are without some representatives.

Single-coloured koi

All-red Kohaku are usually culled early in the selection process, but if the hi is of exceptional quality the fish may be grown on as a saleable commodity. They are known as Benigoi or Aka Muji. In such plain koi, good body shape and blemish-free skin are paramount. If a Benigoi has white tips to the finnage, it becomes an Aka Hajiro.

Also thrown up in Kohaku broods are all-white koi called Shiro Muji. Their plain appearance goes against most tastes, but a large example with flawless skin is a sight to behold. There is also a rare red-eyed (albino) variant, which is highly prized.

Kigoi (yellow koi) are a very old variety, enjoying something of a comeback. Males, in particular, can attain lengths of 90cm (36in) or more, though usually not with proportionate volume. The colour (the deeper the better) should be uniform across the back and flanks, shading to a silvery belly. Black-eyed

Kigoi are the most commonly available, but the red-eyed (Akame) fish command a higher price.

Magoi are the koi that started it all – the so-called 'black carp' from which all other varieties were subsequently developed. In fact, their colour is a deep bronze, rather than a velvety black. They are strong, vigorous fish and can grow huge. Most show organisers will not accept Magoi as a true koi variety, but large, scale-perfect examples are bred in Japan and find a ready market as pieces of living history.

Chagoi (tea-coloured koi), plain or Gin-Rin, are bred in shades from pale buff to almost brick red. Fully scaled examples need to display well-defined reticulation, while in Doitsu fish the enlarged scales along the lateral line and the two lines running either side of the dorsal fin should be neat and even. These are the giants among the true koi varieties, and in a heated pond can attain 90cm (36in) in just five or six years. Their understated appearance is a good foil to more colourful koi, but their real appeal is their extreme friendliness; they quickly become hand-tame, which encourages their pondmates to follow suit. Mass production of Chagoi means that good examples are becoming harder to find; also beware of metallic finnage which, although attractive, precludes fish from inclusion in Kawarimono.

The blue-grey Soragoi share the growth potential and friendly disposition of Chagoi.

Few Doitsu koi are assigned to a variety on the basis of their German-type scalation, but in Kawarimono we find two – one being Kumonryu (see page 156), the other Midorigoi. Midorigoi are said to be green, although as they grow, 'greenish

Right: A large, saffron-coloured Chagoi is typically the 'character' fish in a pond, acting as a soothing influence on any younger, more skittish fish. However, Chagoi are greedy and often grow fat.

This composite Chagoi shows the wide variation of colours loosely classed as 'brown'.

KAWARIMONO

Left: In this Gin-Rin Chagoi, the uniform base colour is lifted by a full coat of sparkling scales. Imagine what this koi will look like when it attains 90cm (36in) or more, which Chagoi frequently do.

Unique koi

'One-off' koi, difficult to assign to any single variety or recognisable cross, can be benched Kawarimono as long as they are matt-scaled. Many home-breds fall into this category, but whatever their ancestry, they will never make the grade without good body shape and skin quality. These attributes rarely occur in koi from random, flock spawnings.

yellow' is a more accurate description. They have an almost translucent quality, as though lit from within, and bear a superficial resemblance to poor-quality Doitsu Kin Matsuba (metallic gold koi with pinecone scalation). However, the skin of Midorigoi is always non-metallic.

Matsubagoi (fish displaying 'pinecone' scalation) are mostly grouped in Hikarimuji, the classification for single-coloured metallic koi, even though to Western eyes the dark edging to the scales constitutes a second colour. However, one or two non-metallic varieties belong in Kawarimono.

Aka Matsuba could be described as Asagi (see page 138) lacking any blue. The ground colour is red, each dorsal and flank scale being edged in black. In Ki Matsuba the primary colour is yellow and in Shiro Matsuba it is white.

Kawarimono of more than one colour

Ochibashigure (usually abbreviated to 'Ochiba') result from crosses between Chagoi and Soragoi. Grey is the ground colour, the brown in the best examples forming a Kohaku-like pattern. However, fish for the mass market tend to lean heavily towards one or the other element, and could

Right: The only 'green' koi you are likely to see is a Midorigoi. They are always Doitsu. This one has the typical translucent skin associated with the variety, and particularly well-aligned scales.

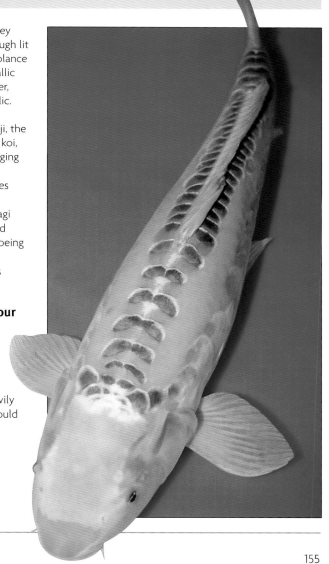

KAWARIMONO

be more accurately described as Chagoi with some grey, or Soragoi with a little brown. Well-defined scale reticulation in non-Doitsu examples is a must.

'Kanoko' means 'dappled'. Instead of having solid hi, some Kohaku, Sanke and Showa exhibit clusters of individually defined red scales, which may or may not be an early sign that the hi is breaking up and disappearing. If it remains, these Kanoko fish are benched Kawarimono, rather than under their own varieties, as clearly they would not be able to compete on equal terms with more conventionally patterned examples.

Kawarimono of Karasu lineage

A Karasu, or Karasugoi (meaning 'crow'), is superficially similar to a Magoi, but the body is a deep, velvety black and the belly can be white, red or orange. Doitsu and fully scaled fish are recognised. From the Karasu have arisen other koi with varying degrees of white on the fins and/or body, and these are named varieties. A Hajiro has a white-tipped nose, tail, dorsal and pectoral fins, which all serve to accent the black body. In Hageshiro, the white extends to the whole head, while a Yotsujiro's fins are completely white. Rarely does a koi fully conform to one of these three sets of criteria nor, provided the effect is pleasing, does it really matter.

The most important koi in this group is the Kumonryu, or 'dragon fish'. It is always Doitsu, always black-and-white, and in the best examples, an interesting wavy white pattern runs symmetrically along either side of the dorsal surface from head to tail. The head may be all-white, all-black or a pleasing combination of the two. Avoid fish with bluish skin, and be

Left: *An Ochibashigure with almost Kohaku-like patterning, resulting from a Chagoi x Soragoi cross. Good scale reticulation is essential in this relatively new variety. Brown on grey is a highly subtle colour combination.*

Right: This is a mature Kumonryu. The patterning on this variety can deteriorate with age, but this example shows the classic 'dragon' sumi (black) running lengthways along the dorsal surface.

Right: An example of an accomplished Hageshiro bred in Israel – proof that good koi are not exclusive to Japan. However, in common with many fish from this part of the world, its body shape lets it down.

KAWARIMONO

aware that young Kumonryu change pattern dramatically as they grow, sometimes for the better, often for the worse.

Matsukawabake are also Doitsu, but with a less well-defined pattern that tends to wrap around the body. This is another unstable variety, whose sumi and white are said to reverse according to the seasons – an oversimplification, as the fish is more likely to turn all-white in high temperatures. In transition periods there are really three colours, rather than two, thanks to the blue-black of emerging or receding sumi.

The fully scaled version of a Matsukawabake is the Sumi Nagashi, with black scales picked out in white. This pattern may cover the whole body, or contrast against areas of pure white skin. Sometimes the tail end of the koi is pure white, and only towards the head is there any black-and-white reticulation.

Kawarimono anomalies

In Japan some koi varieties are placed in Kawarimono, while under non-Japanese show rules, they are benched elsewhere. Prime examples are Goshiki, Koromo Sanke and Koromo Showa (benched Koromo in the West), and Kage Showa/ Kage Utsuri (benched Showa/Utsurimono respectively). The logic is: kage (shadow) sumi may easily be mistaken for emerging sumi, and making a clear distinction is all but impossible, while a Goshiki is only a Koromo in which the robed effect on the pattern extends on to the ground colour. This may occur as the koi ages, so that what is bought as an Ai Goromo later becomes a Goshiki. To save disputes, it is better to bring the two varieties under the same classification.

Early warning system

Who would keep black koi when so many colourful varieties are available? One reason is that their dark skin is the first to show up excessive mucus, which appears as a blue-white bloom in reaction to parasite infestation. So, potentially, they can help to save the lives of their pondmates.

The velvety black skin is much darker than that of a Magoi.

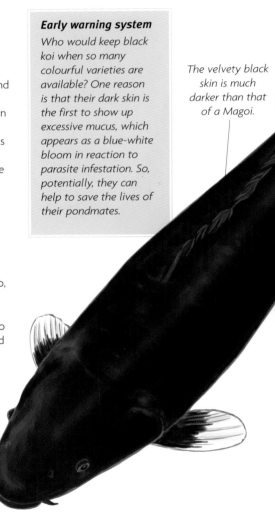

Left: *The distinctive white-tipped tail and pectoral fins mark this fish out as a Hajiro – one of the group known as Karasugoi ('crow koi').*

Right: *Where a third colour, hi, is present, a Kumonryu becomes a Beni Kumonryu – still Doitsu and still non-metallic. The metallic version would be a Kikokuryu, and benched Hikarimoyo.*

HIKARIMUJI

Hikarimuji – single-coloured metallic koi – include the familiar Ogon (formerly spelt 'Ohgon') and the metallic Matsubagoi, whose black scale reticulation is not counted as a secondary colour.

Ogon ancestry can be traced back to 1921, when a Magoi with a gold-striped back was caught from a river in Takezawa, Yamakoshi prefecture, by a gentleman called Aoki. Intrigued by this unusual mutation, he set about fixing it, and after four or five generations of breeding and back-crossing to the original fish he succeeded in producing Ginbo and Kinbo. These dark koi with an overall silver or golden sheen are still thrown in modern Ogon spawnings, but are culled as valueless. So, too, are Kin Kabuto and Gin Kabuto. These have gold or silver-edged scales and a distinctive helmet-shaped head marking. Aoki spawned the first true Ogon in 1946 by running a female Shiro Muji (all-white koi) with eight males from the lengthy experimental breeding programme.

Early Ogon were golden, but with a tendency to turn brownish in warm water. They were known as Kinporai, and reputed to look better in the rain than in sunlit pools – an early attempt at marketing hype. Purer and more stable coloration was established when one of these Ogon was crossed with a Kigoi, a very old koi variety. Modern yellow Ogon are known as Yamabuki Ogon.

Rivalling them for beauty are silver-white koi with a deep, dull metallic lustre. These Platinum Ogon, or Purachina, arose in the early 1960s from crosses between Kigoi and the silver-grey Nezu ('Mouse') Ogon.

Around the same time, the Cream Ogon became popular. This understated metallic koi, midway between a Purachina and a Yamabuki Ogon, is enjoying a minor revival at the moment, fuelled by enthusiasts who like their koi to be subtle.

Above: *These Purachina (silver-white) and Yamabuki (yellow-gold) Ogon show the desired clear, broad heads, well-proportioned pectoral fins and overall metallic lustre. Note the almost three-dimensional appearance of the scales.*

This Ogon has a graceful and symmetrical body shape for a large fish.

Right: One Japanese word borrowed from the European – 'Orenji' – describes this Ogon with Higoi blood. As in all blends of red and yellow, the exact shade varies between individual examples.

HIKARIMUJI

Orange ('Orenji') Ogon resulted from crosses between Higoi and the original yellow metallics, and later with Yamabuki Ogon. Hi Ogon are recorded, but rarely seen.

What makes Ogon so popular? They grow large, and are friendly and unmissable in the pond. More refined tastes favour Go Sanke, but any collection of mainly Kohaku, Sanke and Showa will be enhanced by a few metallics.

Because these are unpatterned fish, Ogon must be exceptional specimens to succeed in shows, with fine skin, even, blemish-free scalation and a clear, lustrous head. The metallic sheen should extend into all the finnage. As the koi grows and the skin stretches, the lighter leading edges of the scales ideally lend it an almost three-dimensional quality.

Mass-produced Ogon are prone to head discoloration and pectoral fins that are too small for the body. They can easily cross the line between 'voluminous' (which is desirable) and 'obese' (which is not). Make sure any fish you choose has both its pelvic fins — missing fins, a genetic fault, can easily be overlooked.

Gin-Rin Ogon

The combination of metallic and sparkling scales in a good Gin-Rin Ogon can be startlingly beautiful. The hallmark of a good specimen is a clear head showing 'Fuji' (as though it has been sprayed with metallic paint which has then developed tiny bubbles).

Doitsu Ogon

In Doitsu Ogon, the enlarged scales along either side of the dorsal fin and along each flank should be neat and symmetrical, and the same colour as the body of the koi. 'Leather', or completely scaleless, Ogons are still benched Hikarimuji. The dull metallic lustre of a good leather Purachina resembles brushed steel.

Swim gym

Ogon may grow fat. To prevent this, install sub-surface filter return pipework, entering the pond at a 45° angle, flush with the walls and pointing slightly downwards. This sets up a circulating current for the koi to swim against, and 'sweeps' solids towards the bottom drains.

A metallic fish with Gin-Rin scales – an unlikely but effective combination.

Below: A Gin-Rin Orenji Ogon would be an eye-catcher in any pond. When choosing a fish such as this, first decide its merits as an Ogon. The Gin-Rin scalation is an added bonus.

HIKARIMUJI

Matsuba Ogon

Metallic Matsubagoi are benched Hikarimuji. Kin and Gin Matsuba are often seen, not so Orenji and Aka Matsuba (red koi with dark scale reticulation). The pinecone scalation in all these must be well defined, although fish straddling the line between ordinary and Matsuba Ogon are very common.

In Doitsu Matsuba Ogon, the black German scales are aligned as usual, either side of the dorsal fin and along each flank, where they contrast sharply with the metallic body. The orange variety, also known as Mizuho ('Rice Ear') Ogon, is particularly striking.

Below: This Kin Hi Matsuba is a good, though not perfect, example of its variety. The dark nostrils and eye patches let it down, although the head is otherwise clear, with a good lustre.

Scale perfect

Because even minor scale damage will render an Ogon valueless for showing, both fully scaled and Doitsu fish should be kept in ponds where there is no chance of the koi bumping into obstructions and injuring themselves. This is where gravity filtration scores over pump-fed systems – there is no 'hardware' in the pond to injure fish.

The scale reticulation on this koi runs down over the flanks, as it should.

Are the pectoral fins of this koi too small for its body? This is a common fault in Hikarimuji.

Above: *A Doitsu Kin Matsuba looks worlds apart from its fully scaled counterpart. The stray scales running past the gill covers are a fault, and perhaps the metallic lustre is not sufficiently uniform throughout the finnage.*

HIKARIMOYO

Metallic koi of more than one colour are benched Hikarimoyo (abbreviated from Hikarimoyo-Mono), and result from crossing Ogon, Kin and Gin Matsuba with matt-scaled varieties. This very diverse group excludes metallic Utsuri or Showa, which are benched Hikari Utsuri.

The brash appeal of even poor examples of Hikarimoyo can blind purchasers to their defects – they are koi with seemingly limitless colour permutations and a lustre gleaming up enticingly through the water. But there is a price to pay; metallic scales can tone down underlying pattern, with the result that sumi appears as dark grey, and red as brownish orange. Another common failing is head discoloration, particularly dark lines running from the eyes down to the nose – a throwback to Gin and Kin Kabuto ancestry.

Hariwake

To beginners, Hikarimoyo can only mean Hariwake. These koi display two metallic colours: a platinum base overlaid with either yellow-gold (Yamabuki) or orange (Orenji) markings. Where the second colour is red, a fully scaled fish of this type is known, rather confusingly, as a Sakura Ogon – really a metallic Kohaku – while its Doitsu equivalent is a Kikusui ('water chrysanthemum'), again a platinum fish with overlaid hi. It is not always easy to draw the line between red and orange-red, but it makes no difference to the benching of these koi.

The best fully scaled Hariwake show a lot of metallic white on the body, a Kohaku-like pattern and a clear head, although interesting head patterns are also permissible.

The mirror scales of Doitsu Hariwake should be bilaterally symmetrical and evenly spaced. Inferior examples can show coarse scalation all over the caudal peduncle or overly large, coarse scales that impart an unwanted armoured appearance.

In fully scaled Hariwake Matsuba, the dark pinecone insertion point to each scale can appear faded due to the metallic overlay. However, in Hariwake Matsuba Doitsu, the only dark

On Doitsu fish without flank scales, the path of the lateral line can be clearly traced.

Right: *A Yamabuki Hariwake Doitsu. This example has even dorsal scalation, a Kohaku-like pattern and a clear head, all of which combine to give the koi a bright, clear-cut look.*

Right: *This Kikusui shows a pleasing Inazuma orange pattern balanced by a nose spot. However, the fish lacks volume and the Doitsu scales over the shoulder are rather coarse.*

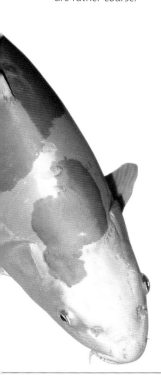

HIKARIMOYO

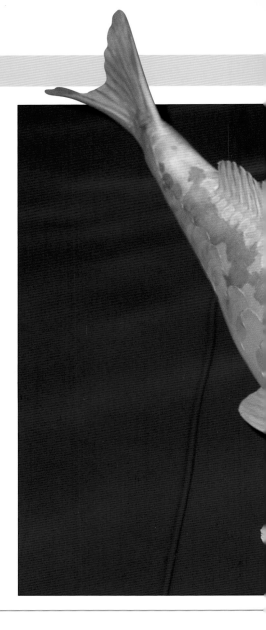

scales are those along the back and flanks, giving a clear-cut impression. These koi can be confused with Midorigoi if their metallic lustre is not strong.

The Tora (Tiger) Ogon is a Yamabuki Ogon crossed with a Shiro Bekko – a yellow metallic koi with sumi as its second colour. The silver equivalent is a Gin Bekko, a cross between a Shiro Bekko and a Platinum Ogon.

Metallic Sanke are known as Yamatonishiki. They arose in the 1960s from a complex breeding programme involving a cross between an Asagi and a Kin Kabuto and subsequent introductions of Sakura Ogon blood. The darker the sumi and the more scarlet the hi, the better. Lustrous finnage may or may not show sumi stripes, and in all other respects these koi should resemble true Sanke. A similar-looking fish, the Koshi-nishiki, arose from a cross between a Yamabuki Doitsu and a Gin Showa. The sumi turned out to owe more to Sanke than to Showa lineage, so Koshi-nishiki are now grouped with Yamatonishiki.

Kujaku (or Kujaku Ogon) were first bred in 1960 from Shusui, Kin Matsuba and Hariwake parentage. The result was a metallic platinum fish with black Matsuba scalation overlaying hi, a clear red head, and some blue derived from the female brood koi. Many of these first Kujaku (meaning 'peacock') were Doitsu, from the Shusui influence. Like Goshiki, Kujaku are said to be five-coloured koi, but not all modern fish display white, black, red, brown and yellow. For example, a subvariety, the Beni Kujaku, is predominantly red.

Judging standards for modern Kujaku have become quite flexible. An interesting head pattern is just as acceptable as plain red, yellow or platinum. Still important is a good, even Matsuba pattern from head

Left: *A Doitsu Lemon Hariwake showing the typical 'linear' scale pattern on the dorsal surface and flanks. The secondary colour on this fish is pale yellow, hence the common name for this variety.*

Note the perfect pectoral fins on this example.

Left: *This fully scaled Orenji Hariwake is not far removed from the variety known as a Sakura Ogon – but the pattern is definitely orange, rather than red.*

169

HIKARIMOYO

to tail, and a deep lustre extending into all the finnage. Of all the Hikarimoyo, the Japanese value Kujaku the most highly, because it is so difficult to breed fish that display all the required attributes.

Doitsu Kujaku are sometimes mistaken for the metallic Shusui x Ogon crosses, Ginsui and Kinsui. The difference is in the positioning of the hi which, in the latter, covers the cheeks and flanks, rather than the dorsal surface.

Metallic Ai Goromo (Shochikubai) are quite rare. The reticulated hi is more brown than red, forming a subtle counterpoint to the silver skin.

Given that breeders are understandably tempted to try all permutations of metallic and non-metallic koi to see what arises, Hikarimoyo attracts more than its fair share of new koi varieties. An example is the Kikokuryu, a Doitsu metallic with a helmet-like head pattern not unlike that of a ghost koi. It is over-simplistic to dismiss it as a metallic Kumonryu, because black and silver are not the only colours – hi may also be present, from the black and red fish known as Beni Kumonryu.

Another new 'variety' that has yet to achieve much popularity is the Heisei-Nishiki – a Yamatonishiki-like koi whose sumi markings owe more to Showa than Sanke without moving it into Kin Showa territory.

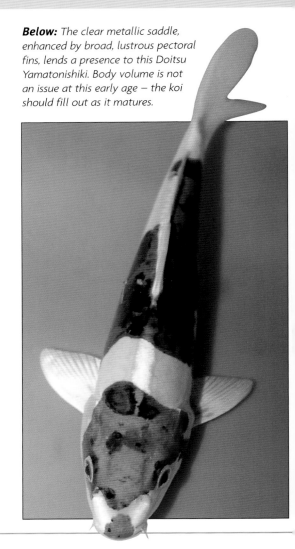

Below: *The clear metallic saddle, enhanced by broad, lustrous pectoral fins, lends a presence to this Doitsu Yamatonishiki. Body volume is not an issue at this early age – the koi should fill out as it matures.*

The first breeder of Yamatonishiki, Seikichi Hoshino, took 15 years to develop it.

Above: A pair of Yamatonishiki, which give a 'feel' for this variety, even though the patterning is very different. See how the sumi is toned down in these metallic koi, suggesting that more can actually be less.

HIKARIMOYO

Right: Were it not for the telltale reticulated mirror scales along the dorsal surface, this Doitsu Kujaku would pass for a Doitsu Hariwake. The pinecone Matsuba scalation is all that sets apart the two varieties.

Left: A very subtly marked Shochikubai (metallic Ai Goromo). Hikarimoyo need not be brash to be good, and the pattern and skin quality of this fish put it right in among the best Go Sanke. The robing over the hi will develop further with age.

Left: This Kujaku has good scale reticulation and a pleasing, if rather unusual, intrusion of hi into the head. The nose spot, too large to be a mere blemish, enhances rather than detracts from the overall impression.

Clear, lustrous pectoral fins adjoin pure white shoulders in an acceptable break to the pattern that adds to an impression of girth where it is most needed.

173

HIKARI UTSURI

Hikari Utsuri (metallic Showa and Utsurimono x Ogon crosses) proved tremendously popular when they first reached the West. Now their appeal is on the wane, as evidenced by dwindling show entries into this class. It may be that hobbyists are more sophisticated in their appreciation of koi, but more likely, the fall from grace of Hikari Utsuri can be blamed on the toning down of hi and sumi that occurs whenever it is overlain with metallic scales. In all but the very best examples, this results in koi that look washed out.

Running parallel with this situation is the huge improvement in the quality of matt-scaled Showa and Utsurimono, which need no further gilding to stand out in the pond. Breeders are now back-crossing Hikari Utsuri to the non-metallic side of the partnership in an effort to intensify the hi and sumi while still retaining full lustre.

For some reason, all metallic Showa are known as Kin Showa; there is no such thing as a Gin Showa, even though the koi's prevailing skin colour may be silver. However, Kin and Gin Matsuba are recognised varieties in Hikarimuji.

Kin Showa

First and foremost, Kin Showa should measure up to all the usual Showa attributes. Key elements include wraparound sumi, motoguro in the pectoral fins, and an interesting black pattern travelling through the head. Hi and sumi should not tail away, and there must be no congenital mouth or

Butterfly outcasts

Koi varieties are determined by colour, pattern, type and scale configuration and whether they are matt or metallic. Their shape has not been modified – with one exception. Long-finned, or butterfly, koi have elongated finnage and barbels. There is no show category for them, and the Japanese do not acknowledge them.

Left: A Tategoi (young fish with potential) Kin Showa with marvellous skin and plenty more sumi still to come through. If the black pattern eventually crosses the lustrous face, so much the better. Buying Tategoi is an exciting gamble.

Right: This Kin Showa's hi is toned down by the metallic skin, but the sumi is holding its own. Motoguro fans out into the pectoral fins and balances the koi. The head sumi still has more to do.

175

HIKARI UTSURI

spine deformities. The hi should be dark crimson, rather than the brown it often is, and the sumi as near black as possible. Showa sumi is stronger than that of Sanke, and holds its own better in metallic fish.

All modern Showa pattern variations are permitted in Hikari Utsuri. Metallic Kindai Showa, where white (now silver) predominates, make especially bright koi.

Gin Shiro

A metallic Shiro Utsuri is called a Gin Shiro (Gin Bekko are benched Hikarimoyo). The contrast between the black and white areas is toned down, but more apparent in the Doitsu version. The modern taste for smaller areas of sumi suits these koi best, and all-white pectorals, or those with neat motoguro, show off lustre to better advantage than dark finnage.

Kin Hi Utsuri

Kin Hi Utsuri are arguably the most successful Hikari Utsuri. In these metallic Showa, which lack any white, the hi in good specimens remains bright crimson, while the pectoral fins – candy-striped black and silver with a golden overlay – can practically glow. Head sumi is not generally as well defined as in Shiro Utsuri, and dark nostrils on an otherwise all-red head are a common fault.

Kin Ki Utsuri

The final fish in this classification is the Kin Ki Utsuri – a metallic yellow koi with wraparound sumi. It is usually described as a cross between Ki Utsuri and Ogon, but a more credible parentage would be Yamabuki Ogon/Shiro Utsuri. Matt-scaled Ki Utsuri, although a very old variety, are now hardly ever seen in the hobby.

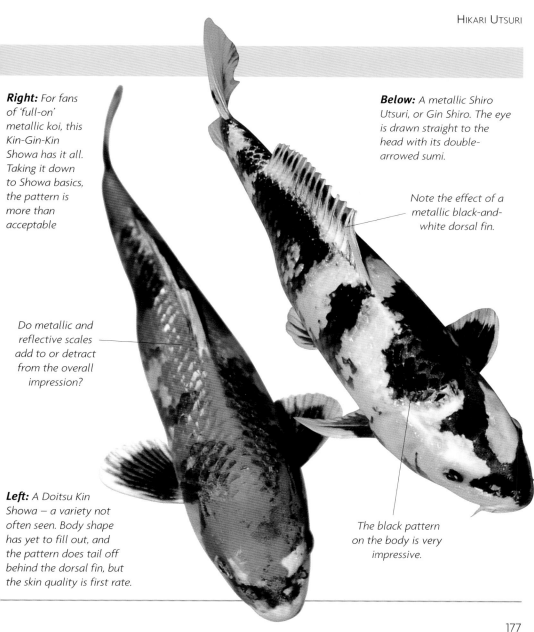

Right: For fans of 'full-on' metallic koi, this Kin-Gin-Kin Showa has it all. Taking it down to Showa basics, the pattern is more than acceptable

Below: A metallic Shiro Utsuri, or Gin Shiro. The eye is drawn straight to the head with its double-arrowed sumi.

Note the effect of a metallic black-and-white dorsal fin.

Do metallic and reflective scales add to or detract from the overall impression?

Left: A Doitsu Kin Showa – a variety not often seen. Body shape has yet to fill out, and the pattern does tail off behind the dorsal fin, but the skin quality is first rate.

The black pattern on the body is very impressive.

HIKARI UTSURI

The bright golden ground colour on good specimens is overlain with Showa-type sumi. The scales appear dark where they enter the skin, blackish gold in the centre, and dark again at the rim – a very subtle and pleasing effect. Any kage (shadowy) patterning that remains into adulthood will not affect the benching of these koi, although it may work against them when they are judged.

Gin-Rin Kin Ki Utsuri offer the added sparkle of reflective scales over a metallic base, but the sumi needs to be very strong to work through this combination. When it does – and as long as the pattern holds up in all other respects – a stunning koi is the result.

Metallic mongrels

Crosses between normally and metallic-scaled koi can result in attractively patterned pond fish of uncertain lineage. However, all such 'mongrels' (usually home-bred) are still placed in Hikari Utsuri or Hikarimoyo, rather than in Kawarimono, because the latter classification does not include metallics.

Left: A metallic yellow koi with Showa-style sumi is known as a Kin Ki Utsuri. This one has sparing sumi and the candy-striped pectoral fins that sometimes replace motoguro.

A broad head and 'chubby cheeks' are characteristics of mature koi, rather than youngsters.

Right: Black on red, with a golden metallic glow, makes a good Kin Hi Utsuri the king of Hikari Utsuri. This variety is prone to shimis, but there are few such blemishes on this particular example.

KIN-GIN-RIN

Gin-Rin scales are quite distinct from those of metallic koi, although koi such as Gin-Rin Ogon exhibit both types. The flat gleam of metallic scales is caused by the reflective pigment guanine. Kin-Gin-Rin (usually abbreviated to Gin-Rin) scales, on the other hand, have a sparkling deposit over all or part of their surface and, depending on type, may be flat or convex. When they overlay sumi or white they appear silver (Gin), while over hi the effect is golden (Kin). 'Gin-Rin' is frequently mispronounced. The 'G' should be hard, as in 'gate', not soft, as in the spirit mixed with tonic.

Individual sparkling scales first appeared in 1929, on fish owned by breeder Eizaburo Hoshino. He named them 'Gingoke' – another term is 'Dia'. To qualify as Gin-Rin today, a koi should have too many of these scales to be counted accurately as it swims past the observer. The cut-off point is approximately 20. Fewer than that on an otherwise matt-scaled koi can still look very attractive and do not detract from its value.

In any case, in the West only Gin-Rin Go Sanke are benched Kin-Gin-Rin. In Japan, Kin-Gin-Rin 'A' covers Go Sanke, and Kin-Gin-Rin 'B' covers all other koi with scales of this type.

If the sparkling deposit is heavy enough, the central area of the scales will feel slightly raised, like the dimples on a golf ball. This is Pearl, or Tsubo, Gin-Rin, also known as Tama-Gin.

The three forms of flat Gin-Rin

Flat Gin-Rin occurs in three forms. In Beta-Gin, the whole surface of the scale sparkles. Beta-Gin is usually found on the abdomen, along the lateral line or in individual rows towards the dorsal surface. In Kado-Gin, only the leading edge carries the glistening pigment. The third type, Diamond or Hiroshima Gin-Rin,

Above: Anyone would be proud to own this impressive Gin-Rin Sanke. The white saddle with tsubo sumi, the well-placed shoulder marking and neatly aligned sparkling scales all add up to a really class act in koi terms.

Different scales

Diamond Gin-Rin The most striking, yet the least esteemed, form of Gin-Rin is also known as 'Hiroshima Gin-Rin' from its place of origin in southern Japan. It can hide a multitude of sins.

Kado-Gin Only the scales' leading edges are iridescent. The amount of shiny pigment must be uniform across all scales. Gin-Rin should extend over the dorsal surface, although often it does not.

Beta-Gin Iridescent pigment covers the entire scale surface, not just the leading edges. This type of Gin-Rin is often found in 'borderline' fish; ideally it should cover much of the body.

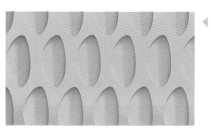

Pearl Gin-Rin Also known as 'Tama-Gin' or 'Tsubo-Gin'. This type of scale looks best on younger koi. The centre of each scale carries a raised deposit of iridescence and gives the skin a 3-D appearance.

Above: This rather plain Gin-Rin Chagoi is 'lifted' by the sparkling coat of scales that overlay the entire body. But it is also a fine Chagoi in its own right.

KIN-GIN-RIN

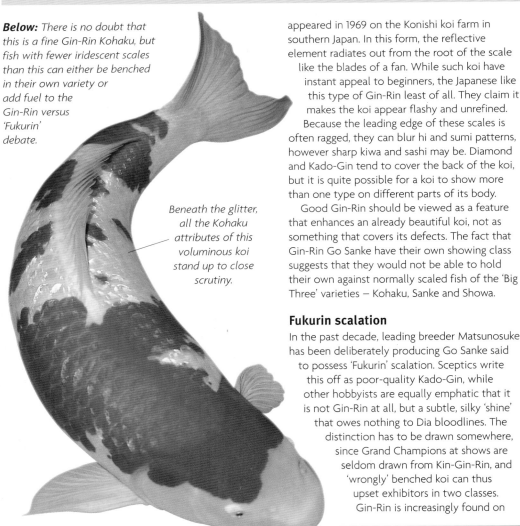

Below: *There is no doubt that this is a fine Gin-Rin Kohaku, but fish with fewer iridescent scales than this can either be benched in their own variety or add fuel to the Gin-Rin versus 'Fukurin' debate.*

Beneath the glitter, all the Kohaku attributes of this voluminous koi stand up to close scrutiny.

appeared in 1969 on the Konishi koi farm in southern Japan. In this form, the reflective element radiates out from the root of the scale like the blades of a fan. While such koi have instant appeal to beginners, the Japanese like this type of Gin-Rin least of all. They claim it makes the koi appear flashy and unrefined. Because the leading edge of these scales is often ragged, they can blur hi and sumi patterns, however sharp kiwa and sashi may be. Diamond and Kado-Gin tend to cover the back of the koi, but it is quite possible for a koi to show more than one type on different parts of its body.

Good Gin-Rin should be viewed as a feature that enhances an already beautiful koi, not as something that covers its defects. The fact that Gin-Rin Go Sanke have their own showing class suggests that they would not be able to hold their own against normally scaled fish of the 'Big Three' varieties – Kohaku, Sanke and Showa.

Fukurin scalation

In the past decade, leading breeder Matsunosuke has been deliberately producing Go Sanke said to possess 'Fukurin' scalation. Sceptics write this off as poor-quality Kado-Gin, while other hobbyists are equally emphatic that it is not Gin-Rin at all, but a subtle, silky 'shine' that owes nothing to Dia bloodlines. The distinction has to be drawn somewhere, since Grand Champions at shows are seldom drawn from Kin-Gin-Rin, and 'wrongly' benched koi can thus upset exhibitors in two classes. Gin-Rin is increasingly found on single-coloured koi, such as Chagoi and Soragoi, 'lifting' them into another dimension. It is a worthwhile attribute, too, on Asagi. Hobbyists who consider the matt version to be somewhat uninspiring may still be drawn to the same koi with an overcoat of sparkling scales.

Reflective silver scales add a new dimension to a great blue-grey fish.

Right: *The increasing popularity of Soragoi (grey koi) is down to breeders producing more of these very understated fish with the added allure of Gin-Rin scales.*

TANCHO

Tancho are very much koi for the purist – the Tancho Kohaku, especially, epitomising the Japanese love of perfection in simplicity. This attribute is apparent in several of their traditional art forms, including Bonsai and Zen gardens, with their stark and symbolic arrangements of rocks and raked gravel. What makes an otherwise pure white koi with perfectly circular head hi even more desirable is that good examples are extremely rare. Usually, either the hi lets a fish down in terms of its depth, shape or position, or else the koi's body is somehow at fault – too fat, too thin, or with disfiguring shimis.

The national bird of Japan is the Tancho crane which, like its namesake koi, sports a round, red head marking. There is an obvious tie-in, too, with the Japanese flag, so Tancho koi strike several emotional chords simultaneously.

Virtually any koi variety can display a symmetrical head marking loosely described as 'Tancho', and this would not even have to be a red patch; for example, it could just as easily be sumi on a Yamabuki Ogon as hi on a Karasugoi. But the only true Tancho are Kohaku, Sanke and Showa. To qualify for Tancho status, the head hi has to be the only patch of that colour on the fish. The term for a koi with stand-alone head hi and red patterning elsewhere on the body is 'Maruten'. Even red lips (Kuchibeni) would make an otherwise perfect Tancho Go Sanke valueless for showing.

Tancho koi can occur in normal, Doitsu or Gin-Rin form. For benching purposes (in Go Sanke only), Tancho overrides Gin-Rin.

Tancho Kohaku

The classic Tancho Kohaku has a circle of crimson hi sited centrally between the eyes. The more perfect that circle, the more valuable the koi. But standards have been relaxed to a point where Tancho Kohaku with oval, crown-shaped, heart-

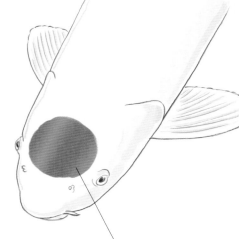

As perfect as they come, this Tancho marking is the right size and shape, and positioned centrally between the eyes of the koi.

Right: *The eye is naturally drawn to the near-perfect hi on this classic Tancho Kohaku, but the fish has other fine attributes – wonderful pectoral fins, good volume and gleaming white skin.*

TANCHO

shaped or other interestingly configured hi are also judged favourably. Whatever form the hi takes, an imaginary line drawn down the centre of the head should perfectly bisect it. Hi slipping down over one eye, like a jauntily worn beret, is fine in Maruten, but not Tancho Kohaku. For every Tancho Kohaku worth the name, many Shiro Muji, and fish with inferior head hi, will result. Other koi, with small additional patches of body hi, are neither good Tancho nor good conventional Kohaku.

Tancho Sanke

Tancho Sanke have head hi complemented by Bekko-type sumi markings on the body and in some or all of the fins. Although small patches of sumi are permissible on the head of a normal Sanke, a Tancho Sanke's hi should sit on a clear white ground. Many Bekko are thrown from spawnings of this tricky variety.

Tancho Showa

The third type of Tancho koi is really a Shiro Utsuri with additional head hi, but is known as a 'Tancho Showa'. In these fish, the hi is usually cut through by sumi in a classic menware or V-shaped pattern. More wraparound sumi is present on the body. Such koi are less subtle than Tancho Kohaku because their Shiro Utsuri patterning alone is sufficient to delight the eye. The hi is a bonus – a setting sun crossed by the first clouds of night.

The effects of stress

Koi vary greatly in their reaction to being shown. Some take it in their stride, while others are badly stressed by the experience. When this happens, tiny capillary blood vessels under the skin rupture, turning white areas pink. This is especially noticeable on koi in the Tancho classification, and can wreck their chances. Equally frustrating are koi that lose their head hi soon after purchase. The owner of many a Shiro Muji is waiting – usually in vain – for it to return to Tancho Kohaku status.

Tancho tampering
It is not unknown for Tancho koi to be 'doctored' to improve the uniformity of the head marking. This is done by cryo-surgery, and careful inspection will usually reveal the site of the tampering. Rogue individual red scales on the body of Tancho Kohaku can likewise be bleached or scratched off, so let the buyer beware!

Below: *Unique Tancho markings deviate considerably from the plain circular spot, and this crown-shaped adornment falls into that category.*

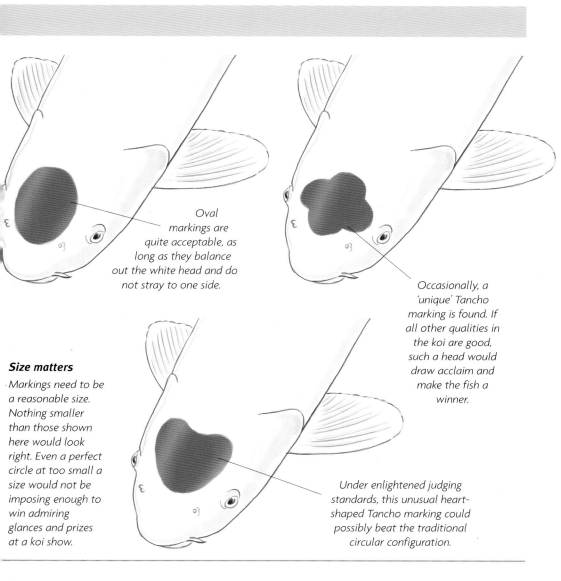

Oval markings are quite acceptable, as long as they balance out the white head and do not stray to one side.

Occasionally, a 'unique' Tancho marking is found. If all other qualities in the koi are good, such a head would draw acclaim and make the fish a winner.

Size matters

Markings need to be a reasonable size. Nothing smaller than those shown here would look right. Even a perfect circle at too small a size would not be imposing enough to win admiring glances and prizes at a koi show.

Under enlightened judging standards, this unusual heart-shaped Tancho marking could possibly beat the traditional circular configuration.

TANCHO

Right: In Tancho Sanke, the sumi as well as the head hi must be well placed. This is certainly the case here, and although the Tancho marking flattens towards the nose, it is still nicely symmetrical. If there were any hi on the body of either of the fish shown on these pages, they would cease to be true Tancho.

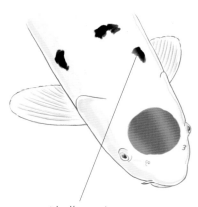

Ideally, sumi on Tancho Sanke should start well back from the head.

Right: The pattern on this Tancho Showa tails off a little, and the head hi wanders over to one eye. Nonetheless, this voluminous koi shows classic head sumi and pectoral fins, and the hi is not overwhelmed but complemented by the intrusion of black.

In Tancho Showa, head sumi striking through hi is quite acceptable.

DOITSU

Today, the word 'mutant' is so much tied in with science-fiction writing that it carries monstrous associations — yet all koi owe their existence to spontaneous genetic changes. Mutations were responsible for the first red or white scales on ancestral black carp bred for food by the Japanese, and later, in Europe, for aberrant scale patterns.

Doitsu scalation must be neat and even, right along the dorsal surface to the tail.

   In the wild, mutations are rarely successful because they tend to work against the survival of the animal or, at best, do nothing to enhance its chances of reaching sexual maturity. For example, albinism (where the black pigment melanin is absent) makes fish especially vulnerable to predators. Even if a mutant wild fish does manage to spawn, there is a bottomless gene pool out there to 'dilute' any new physical or behavioural traits and prevent them becoming mainstream. Evolution is a scientific fact, but other than in isolated populations it tends to be a slow process.

Scale mutations

In Europe, producers of carp for human consumption noticed that in any given spawning, some fish would grow much faster than others. These were retained as broodstock in the hope that their offspring would inherit the trait and, indeed, some did. However, this selective breeding programme also resulted in carp whose scales were very different to the norm. So-called 'mirror' carp have a variable number of enlarged and often reflective scales. 'Leather' carp are practically naked, while linear carp have a double row of scales on the dorsal surface and a single row following the path of the lateral line.

   As well as being easy to prepare for the table, the fast-growing linear carp have played a part in the development of koi. 'Doitsu' (German-scaled) fish came to Japan in about 1907 and were spawned with normally scaled koi. The earliest crossings resulted in Shusui, which are simply Doitsu Asagi.

Left: *Doitsu Kin Matsuba, a variety that can cause considerable identity confusion. The metallic lustre on this example is particularly good. Note how the shoulder scalation differs from that of the Midorigoi shown on page 192.*

Right: *In the West, Shusui are the only named Doitsu fish to have their own show classification, which they share with fully scaled Asagi. With this amount of red, the fish pictured here would be known as a Hi Shusui.*

DOITSU

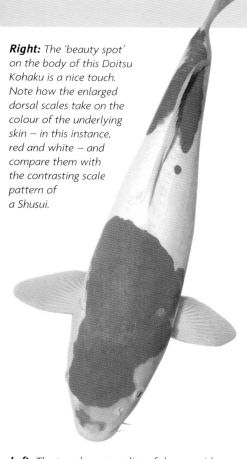

Right: The 'beauty spot' on the body of this Doitsu Kohaku is a nice touch. Note how the enlarged dorsal scales take on the colour of the underlying skin – in this instance, red and white – and compare them with the contrasting scale pattern of a Shusui.

Left: The translucent quality of the greenish yellow skin of this Midorigoi is typical of this rather rare variety. In response to demand, more of these koi are now being bred, but bear in mind that they tend to turn a muddy greenish brown as they mature.

The Doitsu genetic input is a mixed blessing in koi bred primarily for colour and/or pattern, for while a pure-scaled x linear-scaled cross theoretically produces a 50:50 split, parent koi are likely to be of mixed heritage and an indeterminate number of Doitsu fish will be thrown in any spawning. It is even possible for fully scaled parent koi carrying a recessive gene to produce linear-scaled koi, and this is not always what the breeder wants.

The Japanese regard Doitsugoi as rather vulgar and two-dimensional, while still recognising the worldwide demand for them. Without many scales to diffuse the light or blur the boundaries between adjoining colours, these koi can appear chic and almost hand-painted.

Doitsu show classes

In Japan there is a Doitsu show classification for Go-Sanke only, while in the West all German-scaled fish, except Shusui, are judged alongside their fully scaled counterparts. Only a few Doitsu varieties are named in their own right – they include Kumonryu and Midorigoi (benched Kawarimono) and the metallic Kikokuryu, Kinsui and Ginsui (Hikarimoyo).

Some Doitsu fish look startlingly different from their normally scaled counterparts. Ki Matsuba Doitsu clearly lack pinecone scalation and are much more like matt Kinsui, while Ai Goromo Doitsu have clear hi with only blue-black dorsal scales overlaying the red pattern. The traditional 'robing' effect is absent.

It is debatable whether any Doitsu koi can be fairly judged against fully scaled fish. At top show level, a Doitsu Kohaku would never beat a fully scaled koi of the same quality, but that does not make it a lesser fish. A Doitsu 'A' class for Go Sanke and Doitsu 'B' for the rest would be one solution.

DOITSU

Choosing Doitsu koi

When choosing Doitsu koi, look for neat and evenly placed scalation. The enlarged scales on either side of the dorsal fin should match up left and right, while those on the shoulder should form a pleasing arrangement without being too coarse and overwhelming. There should be no stray mirror scales on the flanks or belly.

There is a type of Doitsu koi known as a 'fully scaled mirror', where the whole body is covered by enlarged scales. These can make pretty pond fish, but are valueless for showing.

Leather koi (also classed as Doitsu) are almost completely scaleless, and this configuration works especially well on metallics, such as Doitsu Purachina. Having a naked or near-naked skin is no handicap to a koi, except that any enlarged scales are prone to catching on obstructions in the pond. Infection can then set in within the scale pocket, and if this results in the scale being lost or removed, the essential symmetry will be lost.

Right: *A young and accomplished Doitsu Goshiki of the modern type, with large areas of white skin. The clear pectoral fins are a major plus point. It will be interesting to see how this fish looks when it is bigger – will more dark pigment appear? The potential for change is one of the ongoing fascinations of koi-keeping.*

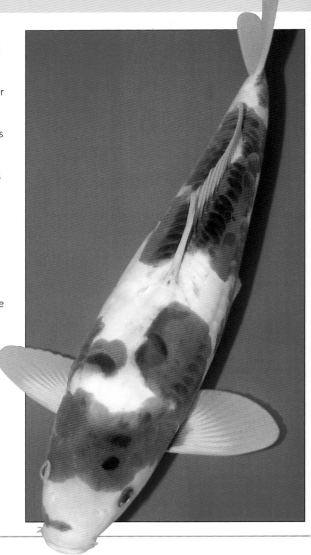

Above: *If Picasso had been asked to paint a koi, he might well have come up with something like this stunning Doitsu Showa. The fish has perfect white skin on which hi and sumi are equal players, while the body shape is particularly good. This is the kind of perfection koi-breeders strive for.*

195

GLOSSARY

Ai Goromo White koi with red Kohaku pattern. Each red scale is reticulated in black or dark blue

Aka Bekko Red koi with black Sanke-type markings

Aka Hajiro Red koi with white-tipped fins

Aka Matsuba Red koi with dark scale reticulation

Aka Muji Non-metallic all-red koi

Aka Sanke Koi with large areas of red unrelieved by cuts in the pattern

Akame Kigoi Red-eyed albino koi

Asagi Koi with a bluish back with reticulated scale pattern. Some red on cheeks, flanks and pectoral fins

Asagi Magoi Forerunner of all modern koi

Ato sumi Black markings that appear later in a koi's life

Bekko Black Sanke-type markings on a white, red or yellow base

Shiro Bekko has no hi markings.

Benigoi Non-metallic, deep crimson koi

Beni Kujaku Predominantly red sub-variety of Kujaku

Beni Kumonryu Kumonryu in which the normally white areas are replaced by hi – a black and red koi of Karasu lineage

Beta-Gin The whole surface of the scale is reflective

Boke Showa Showa with indistinct greyish black pattern

Budo Goromo White koi with purplish patches of black overlaying red in a pattern resembling bunches of grapes

Budo Sanke Budo Goromo with additional solid black markings

Chagoi Non-metallic brown koi

Dia Mutant scales that appear gold over red, and silver over white areas of skin. *See* Gin-Rin.

Diamond-Gin-Rin Reflective pigment that radiates out in a fan shape

Doitsu Koi with no scales other than enlarged scales along the lateral line and two lines running either side of the dorsal fin

Doitsu Ai Goromo The only blue/black scales are the enlarged ones running along the back

Doitsu Hariwake Platinum koi with metallic yellow (gold) markings

Fuji Metallic lustre with tiny bubbles

Fukurin Net effect of lustrous skin around the scales of (usually) metallic koi

Gin Silver

Gin Bekko Cross between a Shiro Bekko and a Platinum Ogon

Ginbo Dark koi with an overall silver sheen

Gin Kabuto Black helmeted koi with silver edges to scales

Gin Matsuba Metallic silver with pinecone scalation

Gin-Rin Koi with reflective silver scales

Diamond Gin-Rin scales are bold but can blur hi and sumi patterns.

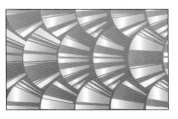

Gin Shiro Metallic Shiro Utsuri

Ginsui Metallic Shusui with a silver lustre

Godan Five-step pattern

Go Sanke Koi from the Kohaku, Sanke and Showa classes

Goshiki Koi with five-colour pattern made up from red, white, black, light blue and dark blue

Goshiki Shusui Doitsu, non-metallic blue Goshiki

Hageshiro Black koi with white on the head and white-tipped pectoral fins

Hajiro Black koi with white tail tip and white-tipped pectoral fins

Hana Shusui Red in a wavy pattern to give a flowery effect

Hariwake Two-coloured koi with platinum base overlaid with orange or gold

Heisei-Nishiki Doitsu Yamatonishiki with sumi all over the body

Hi Red

Hi Asagi Asagi in which red patterning extends almost up to the dorsal fin

Higoi Red koi

Hikarimoyo Class for all multicoloured metallic koi except Utsuri and Showa

Hikarimuji Class for single-coloured metallic koi

Hikari Utsuri Class for metallic Utsurimono and Showa

Hiroshima Gin-Rin Reflective pigment that radiates out in a fan shape

Hi Showa More than half the body viewed from above is red

Hi Shusui Red extends up over the back contrasting with the dark blue

GLOSSARY

Hi Utsuri Black koi with red or orange markings

Hon sumi Solid Sanke-type black markings

Inazuma Lightning bolt pattern

Ippon hi Where solid red runs from nose to tail without a break

Kado-Gin Scales where only the leading edge carries the reflective pigment

Kage Shadowy black reticulated marking over white (or red on Hi Utsuri)

Kanoko Dappled, like a fawn (usually applied to stippled hi markings on a Kohaku)

Kanoko Kohaku Kohaku with dappled red pattern

Kawarimono includes Chagoi in shades of brown.

Karasu Koi with matt black fins and body and a white or orange belly

Kasane sumi Black that overlays red

Kawarimono Class for all non-metallic koi not included in any other group

Ki Yellow

Ki Bekko Lemon-yellow with black Sanke-type markings

Kigoi Non-metallic lemon-yellow koi

Kikokuryu Metallic Kumonryu

Kikusui Doitsu platinum koi with metallic orange markings

Ki Matsuba Non-metallic yellow koi with pinecone scalation

Kin Gold

Kinbo Dark metallic koi with an overall golden sheen

Kindai White skin predominates

Kin-Gin-Rin/Gin-Rin Koi with highly reflective gold and/or silver scales

Kin Hi Matsuba Rare red metallic koi with pinecone scalation, also known as Aka Matsuba Ogon

Kin Hi Utsuri Metallic black koi with red or orange markings

Kin Kabuto Black helmeted koi with gold edges to scales

Kin Ki Utsuri Metallic yellow koi with Showa-type sumi

Kin Matsuba Metallic yellow koi with pinecone scalation

Kin Showa Metallic Showa with gold lustre

Kinsui Metallic Shusui with a gold lustre

Ki Shusui Shusui with yellow instead of red coloration

Ki Utsuri Black koi with yellow markings

Kiwa Border of red and white at the rear edge of hi patterns

Kohaku White koi with red markings

Kokesuke Semi-translucent

Komoyo Small flowery hi markings

Koromo Sanke Ai Goromo with Sanke Hon sumi

Konjo Asagi Dark blue fish. Forerunner of modern Asagi

The patterns of red and white coloration in Kohaku are limitless.

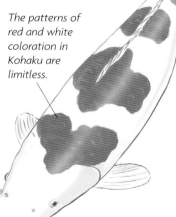

Koromo 'Robed'. Red coloration overlaid with blue or black

Koromo Showa Solid black joins black reticulation over the red

Koshi-nishiki Cross between Yamabuki Doitsu and Gin Showa

Kuchibeni Red lips – literally 'lipstick'

Kujaku (Ogon) Metallic koi with red pattern on a white base and matsuba scalation

Kumonryu Black doitsu koi with some white on head, fins and body

Magoi Ancestral black carp from which all koi were developed

Maruten Kohaku Kohaku with self-contained head marking, plus red elsewhere on body

Maruten Sanke Sanke with self-contained head marking,

plus red elsewhere on the body

Matsuba/Matsubagoi Black centre to scale giving a pinecone appearance

Matsukawabake Non-metallic black and white koi, whose pattern changes significantly with season and water temperature

Menkaburi Red extends down to the nose and over the jaws

Menware Strike-through sumi pattern on head of Showa, Utsurimono or Hikari Utsuri

Midorigoi Greenish yellow koi with mirror scales

Mizuho Ogon 'Rice-ear' Ogon. Another name for Orange Doitsu Ogon

Motoguro Solid black coloration in the base of the pectoral fins on Showa and related varieties

Moto sumi Early sumi that remains on the body

GLOSSARY

Narumi Asagi Asagi with light blue pattern

Nezu Ogon Dull metallic, greyish silver koi

Nibani Unstable secondary red

Nidan Two-step pattern

Nishikigoi Brocaded carp

Ochiba/Ochibashigure Blue-grey koi with a brown pattern

Ogon Single-coloured metallic koi

Ojime A white caudal peduncle

Omoyo Large imposing hi markings

Orenji Orange

Pearl Gin-Rin Reflective, slightly convex silver scales

Platinum Ogon Metallic white koi (also known as Purachina)

Purachina Metallic white koi (also known as Platinum Ogon)

Sakura Ogon Metallic Kohaku

Sandan Three-step pattern

Sanke 'Three colour'. White koi with red and black markings

Sanke Shusui Doitsu Sanke whose pattern is underlaid with the blue back of the Shusui

Sashi Overlap of red and white scales at the forward edge of hi patterns

Shimi Undesirable individual dark brown or black scales on areas of ground colour

Shiro Bekko White koi with black Sanke-type markings

Shiro Matsuba White koi with black pinecone reticulation

Shiro Muji All-white, non-metallic koi

Shiro Utsuri Black koi with white markings

Shochikubai Metallic Ai Goromo

Showa Black koi with red and white markings

Showa Shusui Doitsu koi with intermediate markings showing elements of both varieties

Shusui Doitsu Asagi

Soragoi Plain blue-grey koi

Sumi Black

Sumi Goromo White koi with red patterns lightly overlaid with black

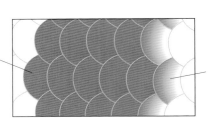

Kiwa, where red scales overlay white.

Sashi, where white scales overlay red.

Sumi Nagashi Koi with black scales picked out in white

Taisho Sanke/Taisho Sanshoku Full names for Sanke

Taki Sanke Asagi koi with white line dividing areas of red and blue on the flanks

Tama-Gin Another name for Pearl Gin-Rin

Tancho Circular red spot on head. No other red on body

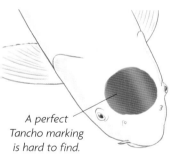

A perfect Tancho marking is hard to find.

Tancho Sanke Sanke with a patch of red confined to the head

Tancho Showa Showa with a patch of red confined to the head

Tategoi 'Unfinished' koi of any age that should continue to improve

Tora/Tiger Ogon Ogon with black markings; metallic equivalent of Ki Bekko

Tsubo-Gin Another name for Pearl Gin-Rin

Tsubo sumi Black on white skin

Calculating pond capacities

To estimate the capacity of various shapes of pond based on their overall dimensions, follow these guidelines.

Square or rectangular ponds:
Volume = length x width x depth. For example, a pond measuring 3.6 x 3 x 1.2m deep has a volume of 13m³ (480ft³). Each cubic metre of water is equivalent to 1,000 litres, while each cubic foot of water is equivalent to 6.25 gallons. The pond capacity is therefore 13 x 1,000 = 13,000 litres (480 x 6.25 = 3,000 gallons).

Round pounds:
First calculate the area of the surface (3.142 x radius x radius). Multiply this number by the depth. Then multiply the result by 1,000 litres/6.25 gallons.

For other pond shapes, divide up the pond into easy-to-measure rectangular, square or circular portions, calculate the volume of each and then simply add them all together.

Using a flowmeter when you fill your pond is the most accurate way of recording pond volume.

Utsurimono Black koi with white, red or yellow markings

Yamabuki Yellow-gold

Yamatonishiki Metallic Sanke

Yondan Four-step pattern

Yotsujiro Black koi with white head, pectoral, dorsal and caudal fins

GENERAL INDEX

Page numbers in **bold** indicate major entries; *italics* refer to captions, annotations and panels; plain type indicates other text entries.

KOI COLOUR VARIETIES INDEX

CREDITS

The publishers would like to thank the following photographers for providing images, credited here by page number and position: (B) Bottom, (T) Top, (C) Centre, (BL) Bottom left, etc.

Shunzo Baba (Kinsai Publishers Co. Ltd., Tokyo): 105(R), 108, 109, 115(L), 140, 157(R), 159, 181

Dave Bevan: 39, 42, 53(T), 79

David Brown: 27, 45(TL), 100

Nigel Caddock, Nishikigoi International: 111, 113, 115(R), 117, 119, 120, 121, 123, 125(T), 126, 127, 128, 129, 133, 136, 142, 146, 147, 148, 151, 153, 155, 156, 157(L), 160-161, 167, 169(R), 170, 172, 173(L), 174, 177(L,R), 178, 185, 186, 189, 190, 192, 193, 194, 195

Eric Crichton: 7(© Interpet Publishing), 35, 37(T,B),

88(© Interpet Publishing)

Steve Hickling: 75(BL,TR)

Terry Hill (The Koi Pond Konstruction Kompany): 38(BR), 56, 58(B)

Andrew McGill: 125(B), 132, 134-135, 141, 143, 149(L,R), 150, 154, 161(R), 162-163, 164, 165, 166-167(C), 168-169, 171, 173(R), 175, 176, 179, 180, 182, 183, 188, 191

Marine World Publications Ltd: 38(BL, Colin and Thelma Shaw), 40 (Bob Lewis), 41(TL, Richard and Donna Jones), 41(BL)

Darren Metalli: 58(T)

Tony Pitham, Koi Water Barn: 74, 76, 77, 102, 103(TL,BL,BC), 116

Will Moody: 103(TR)

Computer graphics (© Interpet Publishing) by Phil Holmes and Stuart Watkinson.

Index compiled by Amanda O'Neill.

The publishers would like to thank the following for their help: Koi Water Barn, Chelsfield Village, Kent; Koi Barn Construction – Darren Metalli; Andy Fletcher; Terry Hill, The Koi Pond Konstruction Kompany; NT Laboratories Ltd., Wateringbury, Kent; Selective Koi Sales, Norwich; Nick Stansfield.

Publisher's note